ENTERING THE

ENTERING
THE
Presence
OF God

MOVING BEYOND PRAISE AND WORSHIP
TO TRUE WORSHIP

DEREK PRINCE

ENTERING THE PRESENCE OF GOD
Moving Beyond Praise and Thanksgiving to True Worship
© 2007 by Derek Prince Ministries–International
This edition by Derek Prince Ministries – UK 2021

This book was compiled from the extensive archive of Derek Prince's
unpublished materials and approved by the Derek Prince Ministries
editorial team.

ISBN 978-1-78263-759-2
ePub: 978-1-78263-757-8
Book code B67

Derek Prince Ministries · www.derekprince.com

Set in Arno Pro by Raphael Freeman MISTD, Renana Typesetting

Contents

Introduction

Beginning in the late 1970s and continuing throughout the '90s, something quite remarkable shaped the course of church history.

A praise and worship revolution swept the body of Christ worldwide as names like Maranatha, Integrity's Hosanna! Music, and Hillsong became household names. Believers by the millions pulled their noses out of dusty hymnals – and lifted faces, hands, and voices heavenward. A new breed of psalmists populated a fresh new songbook with "vertically-oriented" hymns. And it wasn't just "corporate," or group, worship that bloomed in this spiritual spring. Countless quiet times got less . . . well, *quiet*, and much more exciting as people discovered the power of private, personal praise.

This revolution had a forerunner. Underlying and animating this extraordinary phenomenon was what became known as the worldwide Charismatic Renewal of the '60s and '70s – a move in which the work and person of the Holy Spirit were restored to the church in fullness. Wherever the Spirit was given latitude, He took people by the hand and led them into the healing, refreshing presence of the Father.

In the middle of that historic charismatic movement was Derek Prince.

If you are new to Derek Prince, you need to know that he is widely recognized as one of the truly great Christian minds of the twentieth century. He was a British citizen who lived most of the second half of his life in the United States and Israel. He was educated at England's prestigious Cambridge University where he was a contemporary of C.S. Lewis. (How many Bible teachers do you know who have held a fellowship in Ancient and Modern Philosophy at Cambridge?)

In the autumn of 2003, Derek Prince died in his beloved Jerusalem – his home for nearly twenty years. He was eighty-eight.

As you are about to find out on the pages that follow, those amazing intellectual credentials didn't mean Derek's teaching was dry, abstract, or pedantic. He may have had the mind of a philosopher, but God gave him the soul of a free-spirited poet. You will find the teaching of Derek Prince to be inspiring, uplifting, practical, enlightening, always accessible – and never more so than on the important subjects of worship and fellowship with God.

On one of his widely acclaimed radio broadcasts in the 1980s, Derek said:

> I've had the privilege of traveling and ministering in many different countries of the world, and I've been in many places that the Spirit of God was moving and where the Spirit of God was poured out and spiritual gifts were in operation. But I've been in few places where there was true, pure, anointed praise and worship offered to God. When you come to God in spiritual worship, you enter into fellowship with God. Through worship and fellowship you receive revelation. Though I'm not teaching this as a means of getting things from God, it is nevertheless true that when we approach God on the accepted basis with acceptable praise and worship, truly there is no limit to what God will do for us.

Derek Prince was uniquely equipped to bring you truths and insights to help you properly and effectively enter God's holy presence; to explore deeper dimensions in worship; and to find intimacy, strength, power, and impartation in "the Most Holy Place."

Get ready to discover how truly wonderful that place is.

— Derek Prince Ministries

– 1 –

An Attitude in God's Presence

Worship is one of the main themes of the Bible and something of tremendous importance in the life of the believer. Yet, most Christians do not have a clear grasp of the nature of worship. When most churchgoers talk about worship, they are referring to their Sunday morning worship service. They speak of hymns and choruses, and of the congregation standing and singing the planned music for the day. Unfortunately, I fear that in many of these churches very little worship is taking place. If this is the only frame of reference on the subject for the average believer, then they haven't even begun to worship.

In this book, we will examine worship by looking beyond actions and behavior to where worship really takes place: within the heart. We will define concepts like praise, thanksgiving, and worship. We will identify the things that can hinder our worship. And we will describe the progression that will lead us, step by step, into the very presence of God where we may hear His voice and find rest in His arms.

OUR OFFERING

Whenever we come into God's presence, He requires that we bring Him various gifts or sacrifices. These include, but are not limited to, money and material possessions. But, on a higher level, Scripture speaks of various spiritual gifts or sacrifices that God requires His followers to bring Him. These spiritual gifts are thanksgiving, praise, and worship.

We often use these terms interchangeably. I compare them to the colors of the rainbow which are distinct, yet also blend into one another with no absolute lines of demarcation. Likewise, thanksgiving, praise, and worship are distinct, but they naturally blend into one another. Here is how I distinguish them:

Thanksgiving relates to God's goodness.
Praise relates to God's greatness.
Worship relates to God's holiness.

Holiness is in a class by itself. It is the attribute of God that is most difficult for the human mind to comprehend because it has no parallel on earth. We can talk about the wisdom of God because we know wise people. We can talk about the greatness of God because we know great people. We can talk about the power of God because we have seen demonstrations of great power. But, apart from God, there is no earthly example of holiness – it is something unique to God and to those who have received it from Him. I believe that worship relates directly to God's holiness. But because it is hard to understand His holiness, it can be hard to fully understand and enter into worship.

Therefore, worship is the most difficult of these three gifts or sacrifices for the believer to offer in a way that is acceptable to God. Thanksgiving and praise are primarily utterances of the mouth, but worship is primarily an attitude. Thus, it is important to have an understanding of these three terms if we are to be able to make them part of our offering to God.

PRAISE

Praise runs like a golden thread throughout the entire Bible, from beginning to end. Praise is eternal; its origin is in heaven. It is the ceaseless occupation of all the glorious and eternal beings that inhabit heaven, where they enjoy close and uninterrupted access to God Himself. Uninterrupted access calls for uninterrupted praise.

Praise is also associated with the earth since its beginning. In Job 38, God challenged Job with this question:

Where were you when I laid the foundations of the earth?... When the morning stars sang together, and all the sons of God shouted for joy?

(Job 38:4, 7)

What a beautiful picture of the beginning of the earth! It was praise that sent our planet first spinning on its celestial course, and it is the responsibility of God's people on this planet to see that praise continues to mark its course until heaven and earth are no more.

Praise is the appropriate way that we relate to God as King on His throne.

Yet Thou art holy, O Thou who art enthroned upon the praises of Israel. (Psalm 22:3 NASB)

When combined with thanksgiving, praise gives us access to God. We see this in Psalm 100 where the psalmist said:

Enter His gates with thanksgiving, and His courts with praise. Give thanks to Him; bless His name.

(Psalm 100:4 NASB)

Here are two degrees of access. First, through God's gates, and then, through His courts. The psalmist indicates that it is thanksgiving that brings us through the gates, but praise brings us into the courts. This is also beautifully illustrated in Isaiah where the prophet said to God's people:

Violence will not be heard again in your land, nor devastation or destruction within your borders; but you will call your walls salvation, and your gates praise. (Isaiah 60:18 NASB)

God dwells in a place of perfect peace and tranquility. Not only is there no violence or destruction, but there are not even the sounds of violence or destruction. But notice the way of access: all the gates are praise. In other words, the only way into the place of God's presence and dwelling is through praise. Without praise, we do not have access into the outer courts.

THANKSGIVING

*Therefore, since we are receiving a kingdom which cannot be shaken, **let us have grace**, by which we may serve God acceptably with reverence and godly fear.* (Hebrews 12:28, emphasis added)

Here in the *New King James Version* it says, "let us have grace." But the *New International Version* translates the same verse differently:

*Therefore, since we are receiving a kingdom that cannot be shaken, **let us be thankful**, and so worship God acceptably with reverence and awe.*
(NIV, emphasis added)

Actually, each one is a correct translation. In Greek, "to have grace" – the key word is *charis* – is the same as saying "thank you." There is a direct connection between grace and thankfulness. An unthankful person is a person who is outside the grace of God. You cannot be unthankful and be found within the grace of God.

Three of the world's Romance languages, those based on Latin, all retain a direct connection between grace and thankfulness. In French, *grâce à Dieu* means, "thanks to God." In Italian, the word for "thank you" is *grazie*. In Spanish, it is *gracias*. You cannot separate thankfulness from the grace of God. When we say "grace" before a meal, we are really saying "let us be thankful."

There is a beautiful passage in Psalm 95 that depicts the progress into worship. It begins with loud, jubilant praise – a lot louder than some churches would permit.

Oh come, let us sing to the LORD! Let us shout joyfully to the Rock of our salvation.

(Psalm 95:1)

This does not mean loud singing – shouting means shouting. I like that. I think that if there is one thing that is hard for God to accept, it is half-hearted praise. Scripture says, *"Great is the LORD, and greatly to be praised"* (Psalm 145:3). In fact, if you are not prepared to praise Him greatly, don't do it at all.

Let us come before His presence with thanksgiving;
let us shout joyfully to Him with psalms.

(Psalm 95:2)

Notice again the two stages of access: thanksgiving and praise. There is no other way into the presence of God. The next three verses give us the reason why we should praise and thank God. The Bible is very logical. It does not just ask us to thank and praise God; it tells us why.

For the LORD is the great God, and the great King
above all gods. (Psalm 95:3)

Remember I said that it is by praise that we acknowledge God's greatness. So here the word *great* is used twice. The Lord is *"the great God, and the great King above all gods."* We acknowledge His greatness by loud, jubilant, and excited praise. Then we see Him as the mighty Creator.

In His hand are the deep places of the earth; the
heights of the hills are His also. The sea is His, for
He made it; and His hands formed the dry land.

(Psalm 95:4–5)

So we come to Him thanking Him, praising Him for the marvels of His creation. But that is only our way of access. In verse six we come to worship. Praise and thanksgiving are really our way of approach into worship. Then notice, as soon as we come to worship, it is an attitude.

> *Oh come, let us worship and bow down; let us kneel before the LORD our Maker.* (Psalm 95:6)

Here we have passed from utterance into attitude. We began with praise and thanksgiving, but that wasn't the end or goal. When Christians stop with praise and thanksgiving, they have really missed the goal: true worship – which is not an utterance but an attitude.

WORSHIP

When you come into contact with, become aware of, or have a revelation of the holiness of God, there is only one appropriate response: worship. Without such a revelation, we cannot really have worship. We can have a song service, but we do not enter into worship until we have a revelation, however inadequate it may be, of the holiness of God. And the holiness of God is not to be explained. It cannot be defined. It can only be revealed.

This is very important because I think many Christians have the idea that holiness is a set of rules about where you may go, what you may do, and how you may talk and dress. That has nothing to do with holiness. Paul was very emphatic about that in Colossians:

> *Therefore, if you died with Christ from the basic principles of the world, why, as though living in*

the world, do you subject yourselves to regulations –
"Do not touch, do not taste, do not handle," which
all concern things which perish with the using;
according to the commandments and doctrines of
men? These things indeed have an appearance of
wisdom in self-imposed religion, false humility, and
neglect of the body, but are of no value against the
indulgence of the flesh. (Colossians 2:20–23)

This is so profoundly true. The more you focus on the things you must *not* do, the more power they have over you. You think to yourself, *Don't lose your temper; whatever you do, don't lose your temper.* What is the next thing you do? You lose your temper, because you are focusing on the wrong thing. No wonder many people have decided that they want nothing to do with holiness.

Hebrews 12 speaks about the discipline that God as a Father has for His children:

For they [our human fathers] *indeed for a few days*
chastened us as seemed best to them, but He for our
profit, that we may be partakers of His holiness.
(Hebrews 12:10)

Holiness is not a set of do's and don'ts. God is not holy because He has a set of rules in front of Him in order to check His own conduct. Rules have nothing to do with biblical or divine holiness.

ATTRIBUTES OF GOD

Holiness is the essence of what God is. Everything about God is holy. Thus, in order to have an understanding of holiness, we need to have an understanding of who God is and what He is like. Allow me, therefore, to outline some of the attributes of God – what the Bible says God is.

God Is Light

> *This is the message which we have heard from Him and declare to you, that God is light and in Him is no darkness at all.* (1 John 1:5)

God is light. He not only creates light or sends light forth, but He Himself is light.

God Is Love

> *He who does not love does not know God, for God is love.... And we have known and believed the love that God has for us. God is love, and he who abides in love abides in God, and God in him.*
> (1 John 4:8, 16)

God is both light and love. There is a tension between light and love. Light can scare you; love draws you. I think there is a similar tension in our relationship with God. We want to draw close to Him, but we feel uncomfortable entering into that all-encompassing light.

God Is Justice and Judgment

This is absolutely a part of His nature. In Deuteronomy, Moses emphasized this:

> *For I proclaim the name of the LORD: ascribe great-ness to our God. He is the Rock, His work is perfect; for all His ways are justice, a God of truth and without injustice; righteous and upright is He.*
>
> (Deuteronomy 32:3–4)

Many people accuse God of injustice in their partic-ular situation or circumstances. But the Bible says there is no injustice in God. He is totally just; a God of truth. Consider the words of Abraham in Genesis when he was pleading with the Lord about Sodom:

> *Far be it from You to do such a thing as this, to slay the righteous with the wicked, so that the righteous should be as the wicked; far be it from You! Shall not the Judge of all the earth do right?*
>
> (Genesis 18:25)

That is who God is. He is the Judge of all the earth, and He always does right. There is no injustice, no iniq-uity within Him. We are often tempted to believe that God is unjust, but Scripture declares emphatically that this couldn't be further from the truth.

God Is Anger and Wrath

This is something that contemporary Christianity hardly makes room for but is very important. Our God is a God of anger and wrath. Nahum gives a remarkable picture of this:

> *God is jealous, and the LORD avenges; the LORD avenges and is furious. The LORD will take vengeance on His adversaries, and He reserves wrath for His enemies.* (Nahum 1:2)

The Lord is angry. He is furious and He avenges Himself. This is part of God's divine, eternal nature. If we leave this part out, we are not presenting a true picture of God. The book of Revelation gives us a glimpse of God's judgment that will befall the antichrist:

> *Then a third angel followed them, saying with a loud voice, "If anyone worships the beast and his image, and receives his mark on his forehead or on his hand, he himself shall also drink of the wine of the wrath of God, which is poured out full strength into the cup of His indignation. He shall be tormented with fire and brimstone in the presence of the holy angels and in the presence of the Lamb. And the smoke of their torment ascends forever and ever; and they have no rest day or night, who worship the beast and his image, and whoever receives the mark of his name."* (Revelation 14:9–11)

"Tormented ... in the presence of the Lamb." Not exactly the contemporary picture of the gentle Jesus, meek and mild. But it is a part of His divine, eternal character. God

is a judge. Some believe that God is far too merciful to impose eternal punishment on anybody. That is not scriptural. And furthermore, it is very dangerous.

> *For I testify to everyone who hears the words of the prophecy of this book: If anyone adds to these things, God will add to him the plagues that are written in this book; and if anyone takes away from the words of the book of this prophecy, God shall take away his part from the Book of Life, from the holy city, and from the things which are written in this book.* (Revelation 22:18–19)

If anything is clearly written in the book of Revelation, it is that there is eternal judgment. We are reaching a stage in society where we are much kinder to the criminal than to the victim. Why? Because we do not want to be judgmental. Why don't we want to be judgmental? I believe it is because, in our hearts, we know that if there is judgment for someone else, then there is judgment for us.

God Is Mercy and Lovingkindness

The word in Scripture that is translated as *"lovingkindness"* means "steadfast love." In studying this, I have come to the conclusion that what it really means is the "covenant-keeping faithfulness of God." It is God's faithfulness to His covenant – one of His greatest attributes.

In Psalm 51, David was praying during a time of deep distress, when his soul was hanging in the balance. It was his prayer of repentance after his sin with Bathsheba and murder of Uriah had been uncovered.

> *Have mercy upon me, O God, according to Your lovingkindness; according to the multitude of Your tender mercies, blot out my transgressions.*
>
> (Psalm 51:1)

"*According to Your lovingkindness*" is a reference to God's covenant-keeping faithfulness. David was basically saying, "You have committed Yourself to forgive if I meet the conditions. I am appealing to You on that basis." How important it is to be able to approach God on that basis! This idea occurs in various other psalms as well.

> *Praise the LORD! Oh, give thanks to the LORD, for He is good! For His mercy* [His lovingkindness, His faithfulness to His covenant] *endures forever.*
>
> (Psalm 106:1)

God Is Grace

> *Let us therefore come boldly to the throne of grace, that we may obtain mercy and find grace to help in time of need.* (Hebrews 4:16)

There are two things in this passage that you cannot earn: mercy and grace. We first need mercy, but then we need grace. Grace cannot be earned. Religious people have a real problem because they think they have to earn everything. Consequently, they tend to turn down the grace of God. *"Let us therefore come boldly to the throne of grace, that we may obtain mercy and find grace to help in time of need."* We need mercy for the past and grace for the future. It is only by God's grace that we can become the kind of people, and live the kind of lives, that He requires of us.

God Is Power

The whole Bible is full of testimonies to God's power. Let's look at just one example in the Psalms:

> *The LORD reigns, He is clothed with majesty; the LORD is clothed, He has girded Himself with strength. Surely the world is established, so that it cannot be moved. Your throne is established from of old; You are from everlasting. The floods have lifted up, O LORD, the floods have lifted up their voice; the floods lift up their waves. The LORD on high is mightier than the noise of many waters, than the mighty waves of the sea.* (Psalm 93:1–4)

HOLINESS IS THE TOTAL BEING OF GOD

Let me just recapitulate the seven attributes of God: (1) light; (2) love; (3) justice and judgment; (4) anger and wrath; (5) mercy and lovingkindness; (6) grace; and (7) power. I believe God's holiness is all of that. It is the total being of God. *Holy* is the only word that is used three times of God in the same sentence, in both the Old and New Testaments. In Isaiah the seraphim cry,

> *Holy, holy, holy is the LORD of hosts; the whole earth is full of His glory!* (Isaiah 6:4)

And in Revelation, the living creatures and the elders fall down and cry,

> *Holy, holy, holy, Lord God Almighty, who was and is and is to come!* (Revelation 4:8)

I believe there is significance in the threefold repetition. I think holy is the Father; holy is the Son; holy is the Spirit. And no one else is holy. God is unique in His holiness. And we can only understand or become partakers of holiness insofar as we relate to God.

Worship is our response to the holiness of God. Again, when there is no revelation of holiness, there can be no worship. You can have a nice song service. You can have praise and thanksgiving. But you cannot have worship. For when we know the holiness of God in any measure whatsoever, the appropriate response is always worship.

> *Enter into His gates with thanksgiving, and into His courts with praise.* (Psalm 100:4)

We thank God because we are grateful for what He has done. When we praise Him, we are acknowledging

His greatness, but that is not the end. Many of us stop there. We have entered into the courts, but what are we there for? We are there to worship. If we stop after a praise song, we may have had a good time, but we haven't really found the heart and the purpose of God. There is something crying out for more. We desire the presence of the Lord. We yearn to be in direct contact with the living God and to offer Him the only thing we have to offer, our worship. So let's continue our journey and ask the Lord if, by His grace, He will enable us to enter into His presence. For when we are in His presence, we will begin to truly worship.

– 2 –

Our Appropriate Response

Psalms provide us with such an incredibly clear and beautiful picture of true worship. Let's dwell once more on the rich and powerful language of Psalm 95:

> *Come, let us sing for joy to the LORD; let us shout aloud to the Rock of our salvation. Let us come before him with thanksgiving and extol him with music and song. For the LORD is the great God, the great King above all gods. In his hand are the depths of the earth, and the mountain peaks belong to him. The sea is his, for he made it, and his hands formed the dry land. Come, let us bow down in worship, let us kneel before the LORD our Maker; for he is our God and we are the people of his pasture, the flock under his care.* (Psalm 95:1–7 NIV)

There are three successive phases here that I want to examine. First, in verses one and two we have loud exuberant praise and thanksgiving: *"Let us shout aloud to the Rock of our salvation. Let us come before him with thanksgiving and extol him with music and song."* That is loud, exuberant praise and thanksgiving. It is a prelude of sorts.

Then, in verses three through five, the psalmist gives us reasons for praise and thanksgiving. As we have already learned, we thank God for what He does. We praise Him for who He is. Both reasons are included in verse three, *"For the LORD is the great God."* Elsewhere in Psalms it says, *"Great is the LORD, and greatly to be praised"* (Psalm 145:3). His praise must be related to His greatness. Psalm 95 reminds us of what God did, *"The sea is His, for He made it; and His hands formed the dry land"* (Psalm 95:5).

When we come to God in this way, with praise and thanksgiving, our vision becomes focused on God. This is essential for worship, because the great enemy of worship is self-centeredness. As long as we are all wrapped up in ourselves and our own problems and the things that are going on all around us, we are not in a position to worship God.

As I stated in the last chapter, the third phase is found in verses six and seven, where worship is expressed in attitude.

> *Come, let us bow down in worship, let us kneel before the LORD our Maker.* (Psalm 95:6 NIV)

Let me point out two things about these verses. First of all, worship sets us apart as God's people. The reason given for worshiping is, *"For he is our God and we are the people of His pasture"* (Psalm 95:7 NIV). By worshiping God, we declare, by that act, just who is our God. The one whom we worship necessarily and inevitably must be our God. As I will point out later, that is why it is so important that we worship Him and no other. Worship sets us apart as God's people.

Second, worship is our appropriate response to God's tender love and care for us.

> *"We are . . . the flock under his care"*
>
> (Psalm 95:7 NIV)

RESULTS OF WORSHIP

I want to continue in Psalm 95 to what I believe describes the two results of worship and, eventually, the price of failing to worship.

> *Today, if you will hear His voice: "Do not harden your hearts, as in the rebellion, as in the day of trial in the wilderness, when your fathers tested Me; they tried Me, though they saw My work. For forty years I was grieved with that generation, and said, 'It is a people who go astray in their hearts, and they do not know My ways.' So I swore in My wrath, 'They shall not enter My rest.'"* (Psalm 95:7–11)

Here we see two results of true worship, of bowing down and kneeling in the Lord's presence. First, we hear God's voice. We pass from that stage of loud, exuberant praise and thanksgiving into a stage of inner rest, tranquility, and quietness where everything is hushed, where we are still in the presence of God. In that attitude of worship, we can hear God's voice in a way that we can never hear when we are taken up with ourselves and our own problems and perplexities. One of the essential things about worship is focusing on the Lord, turning away from ourselves – as it were, almost merging our identity in His.

It is vital to be able to hear God's voice. In Jeremiah, God emphatically declared to His people,

> *This is what I commanded them, saying, "Obey My voice, and I will be your God."* (Jeremiah 7:23)

That is the simplest statement I know of what God requires. *"Obey My voice, and I will be your God."* Deuteronomy 28 lists all the blessings of obedience, and all of the curses of disobedience. The blessings begin, *"If you diligently obey the voice of the LORD your God,…all these blessings shall come upon you"* (Deuteronomy 28:1–2). The curses begin, *"If you do not obey the voice of the LORD your God,…all these curses will come upon you"* (Deuteronomy 28:15). The watershed is listening or not listening to the voice of the Lord.

Not to shock you, but it is not enough to just read

our Bibles. In John it says, *"My sheep hear My voice, ... and they follow Me"* (John 10:27). You cannot follow Jesus if you do not hear His voice. It is good to read the Bible, but you can do so without ever hearing the voice of the Lord. I believe that worship is the appointed way to come into that attitude and relationship where we really are able to hear God's voice.

The second result is that we enter into His rest. Worshiping and hearing God's voice bring us into a rest that is not possible in any other way. Only those who really know how to worship can really enjoy His rest. (Rest is very rare among contemporary Americans. They are a restless, nervous bunch of people.)

> *There remains, then, a Sabbath-rest for the people of God; for anyone who enters God's rest also rests from his own work, just as God did from his. Let us, therefore, make every effort to enter that rest, so that no one will fall by following their example of disobedience.* (Hebrews 4:9–11 NIV)

Let us consider for a moment the issue of Sabbath rest. I do not preach legalism. I do not believe that Christians are under the Law of Moses. In Romans, we are reminded that, *"Christ is the end of the law for righteousness to everyone who believes"* (Romans 10:4). Christ's death terminated the law – not in its other aspects, but as a means to obtain righteousness. We do not achieve righteousness by keeping the Law of

Moses, and, therefore, I personally do not believe that Christians are required to observe the Sabbath as the Jewish people do.

Besides, even if you could convince me that Sunday was the Sabbath (the Sabbath is to be the seventh day of the week, while Sunday is the first day of the week), we would all be horrible Sabbath breakers. On the Sabbath you are not allowed to kindle any kind of fire, switch on a light, turn on a stove, or travel more than a minimal distance. Most of us break the Sabbath merely by going to church! But the Scripture says, *"There remains therefore a rest for the people of God"* (Hebrews 4:9). I have come to believe that I am not pleasing God if I am busy all seven days of the week.

The first thing God ever sanctified was time. He sanctified the seventh day. Before He sanctified a place or anything else He sanctified time. I believe time still needs to be sanctified. God said to Israel, "Every seventh year you are not to plant anything." (See, for example, Exodus 23:11.) Do you know what that is? It is a test of faith. What are we going to eat, God? "I'll take care of that; you let the land rest." Israel failed. They did not do it. Some centuries later God said, "All right. Your land didn't have its Sabbath; I'm going to change that. You are going into captivity. You will make up for all the Sabbaths that you failed to keep."

I believe that God deals with believers like that, too. Some never rest, week after week, day after day, working away at the same pace, never sanctifying time to God. Eventually, they will make up for all that missed Sabbath with time spent in the hospital.

So I ask you, Do you know what it is to rest? Are you capable of disciplining yourself to stop doing things, even doing them mentally? Can you ever lie down and stop thinking about what you ought to be doing? I'm afraid that many of us don't even know what rest is.

This has been a new concept for me: learning to worship, and learning to rest. I find that they are very closely related. I believe in thanking God and praising Him out loud with dancing, clapping, and singing. But there comes a time when we need to bow down and become quiet. Today, if you will hear His voice, do not harden your heart. Don't miss His rest.

RESULTS OF FAILING TO WORSHIP

Israel, as a people, failed to accept God's call to worship. If we go back and look at Psalm 95, we will see the results of their failure.

Today, if you will hear His voice: "Do not harden your hearts, as in the rebellion, as in the day of trial in the wilderness, when your fathers tested Me; they tried Me, though they saw My work. For forty years I was grieved with that generation, and said, 'It is a people who go astray in their hearts, and they do not know My ways.' So I swore in My wrath, 'They shall not enter My rest.'" (Psalm 95:7–11)

What were the results of Israel's failure to worship? First, their hearts were hardened. Second, they did not hear God's voice. Third, they provoked God to anger. And fourth, they did not enter into their appointed rest. They failed to follow the steps of praise and thanksgiving that lead us into bowing and kneeling down, an attitude of stillness, of hushed reverent quietness before God in which we hear His voice, and through which we enter into our appointed rest.

In 1 Kings 19, it is recorded that Elijah had been running away from Jezebel. He took refuge in the desert and then he made the long journey to Mt. Horeb, the place where God originally made His covenant with the children of Israel. When Elijah was on Mt. Horeb, the Lord spoke to him, and he went through a number of dramatic experiences before receiving a fresh revelation of the Lord.

> The LORD said, "Go out and stand on the mountain in the presence of the LORD, for the LORD is about to pass by." Then a great and powerful wind tore the mountains apart and shattered the rocks before the LORD, but the LORD was not in the wind. After the wind there was an earthquake, but the LORD was not in the earthquake. After the earthquake came a fire, but the LORD was not in the fire.
>
> (1 Kings 19:11–12 NIV)

That is what I call a prelude to worship: the wind, the earthquake, and the fire.

Such tremendous, tumultuous noise and excitement, but it was not worship.

And after the fire came a gentle whisper.
                                    (1 Kings 19:12 NIV)

The *Amplified Bible* says, "*a sound of gentle stillness.*" That is what I want you to associate with worship: a sound of gentle stillness.

When Elijah heard it, he pulled his cloak over his
face.   (1 Kings 19:13 NIV)

What is that? That is worship. Just as angels and seraphs are portrayed in Scripture as covering their faces and their feet with their wings in the presence of God, Elijah covered his own face.

When Elijah heard it, he pulled his cloak over his
face and went out and stood at the mouth of the
cave. Then a voice said to him, "What are you doing
here, Elijah?"   (1 Kings 19:13 NIV)

Elijah came into that place of stillness and reverence in God's presence where God could speak to him. In that attitude, Elijah heard God's whisper, which he wasn't able to hear in any other way. And, through hearing God's voice, if you read the account that follows, he received new direction and strength. He went out a man renewed with a new purpose, new faith, and new courage. He had entered into his rest through worship.

– 3 –

In Spirit and in Truth

Jesus stated the condition of the heart that alone makes our worship acceptable to God in His conversation with the Samaritan woman at the well. The woman began to talk about the rival claims of Jerusalem and Samaria as centers of worship. But when she began to discuss the claims of these two physical, geographical locations, Jesus turned the conversation in a new and unexpected direction.

> *Jesus said to her, "Woman, believe Me, the hour is coming when you will neither on this mountain, nor in Jerusalem, worship the Father. You worship what you do not know; we know what we worship, for salvation is of the Jews. But the hour is coming, and now is, when the true worshipers will worship the Father in spirit and truth; for the Father is seeking such to worship Him. God is Spirit, and*

those who worship Him must worship in spirit and truth." (John 4:21–24)

The words of Jesus to that woman were prophetic. Within a hundred years of that conversation the temple in Jerusalem was destroyed and it became impossible for the Jewish people to worship there. However, before the temple was destroyed, God made alternative provision for His people to worship Him. He transferred the requirements from a physical location to a spiritual condition. The spiritual condition that Jesus stated was *"in spirit and truth."*

God actually seeks worshipers of this kind. This, to me, is one of the most exciting and amazing statements in the Bible: that almighty God is seeking for people to worship Him. Jesus said, "The Father is looking for worshipers of this kind, the kind that worship in 'spirit and in truth.'"

Let us look at these two spiritual, inward conditions that Jesus mentioned. In doing so, I'd like to start with the latter requirement: "in truth."

WORSHIPING "IN TRUTH"

Revelation gives us quite a list of people who will ultimately be excluded from God's presence.

But the cowardly, unbelieving, abominable, murderers, sexually immoral, sorcerers, idolaters, and all

*liars shall have their part in the lake which burns
with fire and brimstone, which is the second death.*
(Revelation 21:8)

Notice the last item on this list: *"all liars."* Liars cannot have access to the presence of almighty God. That is why we have to worship Him "in truth." There is a vivid example of this in the story of Ananias and Sapphira found in Acts 5. They sold some land and brought an offering from what they had sold and laid it at the feet of the apostles. Unfortunately, this offering was not the entire price of the land that they claimed it to be. They had kept back part of the sum. And that cost them both their lives. They just fell down dead one after the other in the presence of God. (See Acts 5:1–11.) Could there be a clearer warning to us that lies and insincerity cannot have access to the presence of God?

Again, in 1 John, this is what the apostle John said:

*This is the message which we have heard from Him
and declare to you, that God is light and in Him is
no darkness at all. If we say that we have fellowship
with Him, and walk in darkness, we lie and do not
practice the truth.* (1 John 1:5–6)

When we come to God, we are coming into the light. There is no room for darkness, no room for reservations, and no room for insincerity. Everything has to be totally open. Notice the phrase, *"we have fellowship with Him."* Fellowship and worship go closely together. Both fellowship and worship require unwavering honesty, sincerity, and openness. We must worship God "in truth."

WORSHIPING "IN SPIRIT"

To understand what it means to worship God *"in spirit,"* we need to grasp the picture that the Bible provides of the total human personality. According to Scripture, the total human personality consists of three interrelated elements: spirit, soul, and body. This is the picture from a prayer by the apostle Paul for the Thessalonian church:

> *Now may the God of peace Himself sanctify you completely; and may your whole spirit, soul, and body be preserved blameless at the coming of our Lord Jesus Christ.*   (1 Thessalonians 5:23)

We know what the body is. The soul is the ego – it is the attribute that says "I will" or "I will not," and "I think" or "I do not think." It is usually identified as being made of three areas: the will, the intellect, and the emotion. These areas are expressed as three simple statements: "I will," "I think," and "I feel." This is extremely simplified, but I think it is a valid picture of the soul in man.

But the spirit really has only one supreme function – to relate to God. It is not the soul or the body that must worship God, but the spirit. But we cannot really understand worship unless we understand the functions and interrelationships of these three elements.

In Psalm 103, David said, *"Bless the LORD, O my soul"* (verse 1). What or who was talking to David's soul? His soul wasn't talking to itself. So who was telling David's soul to *"bless the LORD?"* It was David's spirit. His spirit was on fire because it was in contact with God. His spirit was saying, "We have got to do something about this. Do not just sit there; do something. Get excited. Bless the Lord." The soul is the gear shift of the personality; the soul makes decisions and then orders the body to move. That is the order of things; the spirit deals with the soul, then the soul deals with the body.

Let's look back for a moment to the account of the creation of man as recorded in the second chapter of Genesis:

> And the LORD God formed man of the dust of the ground, and breathed into his nostrils the breath of life; and man became a living being.
>
> (Genesis 2:7)

There are two distinct sources to human personality. One is from above; one is from below. From above there is the breath, the Spirit of God, breathed into man. From below there is man's physical nature, the body made of clay. The union of spirit and clay produces a living soul, a human personality consisting of spirit, soul, and body.

But when man sinned and rebelled against God, his spirit was cut off from fellowship with God and became dead to God. So man was then, in biblical terminology, *"dead in trespasses and sins"* (Ephesians 2:1).

When man turns back to God in repentance and faith, by rebirth, his spirit is renewed and made capable of restored fellowship with God. Once again, we see the principle that fellowship and worship go very closely together. But we have to understand that it is the spirit of man, not the soul nor the body, that is capable of this direct fellowship with God.

So it is through the reborn spirit that man can relate directly to God, person to Person, spirit to Spirit. Jesus said, *"God is Spirit, and those who worship Him must worship in spirit...."* (John 4:24). It is only that same inbreathed element of human personality that comes from God, that spirit, which is able to relate to God directly and to worship God *"in spirit."*

Read the words of the apostle Paul:

> *Do you not know that he who is joined to a harlot is one body with her? For "the two ... shall become one flesh." But he who is joined to the Lord is one spirit with Him.* (1 Corinthians 6:16–17)

Paul was talking about two different ways of one person uniting with another. One is the fleshly way, sexual union: a man with a woman. But the other is a spiritual way, a spiritual union: the spirit of man with the Spirit of God. That is an amazing picture, but it is very clear. Just as intimately as a man can relate with a woman physically in sexual intercourse, so a believer can relate with the Lord spiritually in the communion of worship; that is, worshiping God in spirit. Worship is communion with God. It is intimate fellowship with God. It is direct union with God.

Neither man's soul nor his body is capable of that. It is only man's spirit that is capable of this unique and most precious of all relationships with God, the relationship of union and communion that comes through worship. This is the highest activity of which man is capable – worshiping God in spirit and in truth.

We must get our entire personality in tune with God and responding to Him, as He desires. Your spirit must work through your soul to move your body. That is the way that it works. Therefore, when your spirit wants to worship God, there is not much it can do without the cooperation of the soul and the body. And a spirit that cannot worship God because the soul and the body do not cooperate is an imprisoned spirit. The body for that spirit is a prison, shut up, unable to respond.

That is the problem with many Christians. We give them the Word, but we give them a very incomplete picture of church and of worship. So now when people do experience the real thing they feel strange because we've conditioned people to expect the abnormal.

Fortunately for us, God has provided a road map

of sorts to worship. He has given us a model to follow that will lead us into worship, and therefore into His presence. This model is "the tabernacle."

– 4 –

Your Body: Cleansed by the Blood and Water

The tabernacle of Moses is one of the most remarkable phenomena of Scripture and one that has always fascinated me. It is described primarily in the book of Exodus, chapters twenty-five to thirty, and thirty-five to forty. The fact that God dedicates about twelve chapters of the book of Exodus to the tabernacle indicates to me that it must have tremendous importance.

Every time I study the tabernacle I am left with a deep desire for holiness and for communion with God. That is the result it has on me, and I am sure it is one of the main purposes for which this account is presented in Scripture.

THE WAY INTO THE HOLIEST

The way into perfection, to maturity, to completeness, and to fulfillment is the way into the holiest, which unfolds in Hebrews as in no other book of the New Testament. Here we see that it is scriptural to use the tabernacle as our pattern in seeking God. Indeed, the very phrase *"the way into the holiest"* (Hebrews 9:8) is taken from the type or pattern of the tabernacle.

> *For if He were on earth, He would not be a priest, since there are priests who offer the gifts according to the law; who serve the copy and shadow of the heavenly things, as Moses was divinely instructed when he was about to make the tabernacle. For He said, "See that you make all things according to the pattern shown you on the mountain."*
>
> (Hebrews 8:4–5)

Right there in verse five are the words that indicate that the tabernacle is our example, or *"the copy and shadow of the heavenly things."* It is a material reality that reflects an unfolding spiritual truth. Then, in Hebrews 9, it is mentioned again:

> *Therefore it was necessary that the copies of the things in the heavens should be purified with these, but the heavenly things themselves with better sacrifices than these. For Christ has not entered the holy places made with hands, which are copies of the true, but into heaven itself, now to appear in the presence of God for us.*
>
> (Hebrews 9:23–24)

THE TABERNACLE

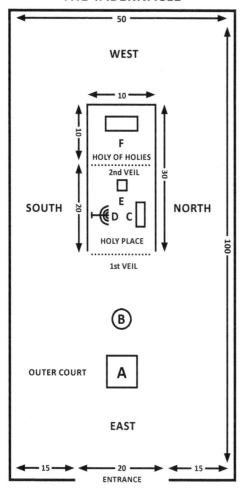

A. BRONZE ALTAR
B. BRONZE LAVAR
C. SHOWBREAD
D. LAMPSTAND
E. GOLDEN ALTAR OF INCENSE
F. ARK OF THE COVENANT

The tabernacle reveals for us a pattern of the way into the holiest, into the presence of almighty God. It is not a matter of groping, or speculating, or simply doing what we please or think. There is an absolutely prescribed way of access into the holiest, and it is revealed to us in terms of the various divisions and the various items of furniture along the way.

The tabernacle was a structure consisting of three main sections: the outer court; the Holy Place, behind the first veil or curtain; and the Holy of Holies, behind the second veil or curtain. It was a triune structure: one structure with three areas. This structure was significant in many ways. It depicted the nature of God – Father, Son, and Holy Spirit. It depicted the nature of the heavenlies – Scripture refers to Paul being caught up into the third heaven. (See 2 Corinthians 12:2.) It also depicted the nature of man – body, soul, and spirit.

One way to distinguish these three areas was by the kind of light that was available. In the outer court the light was natural: the sun by day, the moon and stars by night. In the Holy Place behind the first veil, the light was artificial. It was provided by a seven-branched lampstand. But in the Holy of Holies, behind the second veil or curtain, there was no natural light and no artificial light. The only light was supplied by the supernatural presence of almighty God indwelling that small area within the tent. That presence of God that brings light is known in Hebrew as the *shechinah*, meaning "to dwell" – the visible glory of God. It was the only source of light there in the Holy of Holies, the third area of the tabernacle. It was the manifest indwelling of almighty God in the midst of His people.

These three sections of the tabernacle correspond to many aspects of our experience, but I want to relate them to the three areas of human personality I mentioned earlier: the body, the soul, and the spirit. As I said, we worship God not with the body or with the soul, but with the spirit. So, the outer court corresponds to the body. The Holy Place corresponds to the soul. And the Holy of Holies corresponds to the spirit. It is only in the spirit that we relate to God in worship; therefore, the ultimate area of worship is the Holy of Holies behind the second veil.

So, how does a person progress into worship? By following the pattern found in the progression in the tabernacle from the outer court into the Holy of Holies.

THE OUTER COURT

When approaching the tabernacle, one always began in the outer court. Likewise, when approaching God, we always begin in the physical, natural realm. This area relates to the body and to the life of Christ in the days when Jesus was on earth. He walked the streets of Galilee and Jerusalem as a human being who could be seen, touched, and heard by the natural senses. Thus, in the outer court we receive revelation through the natural senses, or through human knowledge.

In the tabernacle's outer court, the first object one would see was the great bronze altar. A teacher once told me that all its sides were covered in polished bronze, so the moment you approached and looked at it, you saw yourself. This altar was where all of the sacrificial animals were slaughtered and offered to God. For us, the bronze altar represents Christ's sacrificial death on our behalf. It speaks of the blood that He shed, so that we might be redeemed and reconciled unto God. That is the starting point. We cannot bypass the cross. Only when we begin at the cross and receive the benefits of the sacrifice of Jesus on our behalf – the benefits of His shed blood – can we move on in our progression of worship.

Four Sides of the Bronze Altar

The bronze altar had four sides, representing four distinct provisions of God made through the death of Jesus on the cross. The first one is forgiveness of past sins. That is essential. When your sins are unforgiven, you cannot progress any further. This is also stated in Romans:

> *Whom God set forth as a propitiation by His blood, through faith, to demonstrate His* [God's] *righ-*

teousness, because in His forbearance God had passed over the sins that were previously committed.
(Romans 3:25)

The next side represents the taking away of sin. There is an important distinction between *sins* in the plural (sinful acts that have been committed), and *sin* as a spiritual power (an evil, corrupt, enslaving force that causes you to sin, or to commit sinful acts). Sin is the source of sins. When we deal with sins, we are only dealing with the branches of the tree. That does not deal with the trunk that feeds all of the branches of sins. In 2 Corinthians, it says,

For He made Him [Jesus] who knew no sin to be sin for us, that we might become the righteousness of God in Him. (2 Corinthians 5:21)

There is an exchange that occurs. Jesus was made sin, with all our sinfulness, so that in return, we might be made righteous with all His righteousness. That is not *sins*, but *sin* that is dealt with there. We read in Hebrews,

He then would have had to suffer often since the foundation of the world; but now, once at the end of the ages, He has appeared to put away sin by the sacrifice of Himself. (Hebrews 9:26)

43

Christ only suffered once because by that suffering, He did everything that ever needed to be done.

The third side of the altar is our old, corrupt nature – the rebel that is inside each one of us. *"Our old man was crucified with Him"* (Romans 6:6). The Greek here is in the past tense. It is a historical fact. It is true whether you know it or not. But if you don't know it you won't benefit from it.

> *Our old man was crucified with Him, that the body of sin might be done away with, that we should no longer be slaves of sin.* (Romans 6:6)

Sin was rendered inoperative; it no longer was capable of asserting itself. The only escape from the slavery of sin is through the death of the old, sinful nature. The old man is such a hopeless case that God has no remedy for him. God cannot send him to church or teach him the Ten Commandments or make him religious. God merely executes him. That is the only solution for the old man – the old Adam.

The mercy of God is that the execution took place in the person of Jesus on the cross. When Jesus died, our old man died in Him. If you know that, and place reliance on it, it works. But if you do not know it, you cannot place reliance on it, and it will not work. If you know it, but do not place reliance on it, it still will not work. It is the knowing and relying that makes it work.

The fourth side, which is the place where we offer

ourselves to God, is the burnt offering. This was a gift that was offered to God, to be totally consumed in the flames of the altar. If you study the order of the offerings in Leviticus, all of which are symbolic of Jesus, you will find that the first offering spoken of is the burnt offering because the initiative is not with man or the sinner, but with God. (See Leviticus 1:3.) Only because Jesus was made a burnt offering on the altar of God's will on the cross could any of the rest take place at all. If Jesus had not been willing to say, *"Nevertheless, not as I will, but as You will"* (Matthew 26:39), then all the rest would never have taken place.

You will find, in the unfolding of the tabernacle, that we progress in the reverse order from that of Scripture. The Bible begins with the ark and moves outward. That is because the initiative in salvation and redemption is from God, not from man. If God had not been willing, nothing would have ever happened. If Jesus had not been the initial burnt offering on the cross, there would have been no salvation for you or me. But for us, the order is reversed. We must have our sins forgiven; sin has to be done away with, the old nature must die or be crucified, and then we will be able to offer ourselves as an acceptable burnt offering to God. This is brought out in Romans 12:1 which begins, *"I beseech you therefore, brethren...."* The word *"therefore"* refers to the entire unfolding of gospel truth that preceded in the previous eleven chapters.

What does God require of us after all of that has been dealt with?

> *I beseech you therefore, brethren, by the mercies of God, that you present your bodies a living sacrifice, holy, acceptable to God, which is your reasonable service.* (Romans 12:1)

Until you have been on these three sides of the altar, you cannot present yourself as acceptable unto God. Then God says, "I want your body." Few Christians realize this. God wants our entire bodies. In the old covenant, the bodies of the animals that were slain were placed entirely upon the altar. God says, "I want your body on the altar in exactly the same way – with one exception. Not dead, but alive."

The next verse continues,

> *And do not be conformed to this world, but be transformed by the renewing of your mind, that you may prove what is that good and acceptable and perfect will of God.* (Romans 12:2)

Until you place your body upon the altar, you cannot discover God's will. When you do, your mind is renewed and the will of God begins to open up for you. But you cannot make further progress until you have been to the four sides of the altar. First, past sins are forgiven; then God takes them away. Next the old man is executed and the entire body is placed upon the altar in total surrender to God. From then on, your body no longer belongs to you. You are not your own; you were bought with a price. (See 1 Corinthians 6:19–20.)

The Bronze Laver

Next, we find the bronze laver, as described in Exodus:

> *Then the LORD spoke to Moses, saying: "You shall also make a laver of bronze, with its base also of bronze, for washing. You shall put it between the tabernacle of meeting and the altar. And you shall put water in it, for Aaron and his sons shall wash their hands and their feet in water from it. When they go into the tabernacle of meeting, or when they come near the altar to minister, to burn an offering made by fire to the LORD, they shall wash with water, lest they die. So they shall wash their hands and their feet, lest they die. And it shall be a statute forever to them; to him and his descendants throughout their generations."*
>
> (Exodus 30:17–21)

So there was the tabernacle and the altar, and the laver was between them. Attendance at the laver was not optional; it was absolutely required of every person who passed to and from the tabernacle. No one could pass the laver without washing in it. If they did, the penalty was death. Tremendous importance was placed upon the laver.

The laver represents God's Word. Later in Exodus, we read,

He made the laver of bronze and its base of bronze, from the bronze mirrors of the serving women who assembled at the door of the tabernacle of meeting.
(Exodus 38:8)

Brass was taken from the brazen mirrors of the Israelite women who attended and worshiped at the tabernacle. Remember, they had no glass at that time. The best mirror you could have was highly polished, smooth brass. Therefore, we have three aspects of the laver: it came from mirrors, it was made of brass, and it was filled with water. Each one of these qualities speaks to the Word of God.

First, the Word of God is a mirror:

For if anyone is a hearer of the word and not a doer, he is like a man observing his natural face in a mirror; for he observes himself, goes away, and immediately forgets what kind of man he was.
(James 1:23)

God's Word does not reflect the external physical appearance. It shows the inward spiritual condition. If you want to know what you are really like in the sight of God, look in the mirror. The longer I read the Bible, the more I begin to see my imperfection, my flaws, and my inadequacies. When you look into a mirror, you can do two things. You can say that you do not look that bad and simply walk away, doing nothing about it. Or, you can act on what you see, making the necessary changes and adjustments; in which case, James said you will be blessed as a result of what you do. Remember, it is not just the hearers of the Word who are blessed; it is the doers, the people who act upon it.

Second, God's Word is our judge. Brass always typifies divine examination and judgment. God sees you, there is no thing hidden, all things are naked and open unto the eyes of the Lord. In John 12, Jesus said,

> *And if anyone hears My words and does not believe, I do not judge him; for I did not come to judge the world but to save the world. He who rejects Me, and does not receive My words, has that which judges him; the word that I have spoken will judge him in the last day.* (John 12:47–48)

First Peter tells us that God the Father is the judge. (See 1 Peter 1:17.) John tells us that the Father has committed all judgment to the Son. (See John 5:22.) But in John 12, Jesus said, "I am not going to judge you. I have committed all judgment to the Word."

And judgment will be executed by the standard of the Word. It is the absolute standard of divine judgment, which gives us the blessed opportunity to judge ourselves. *"For if we would judge ourselves, we would not be judged"* (1 Corinthians 11:31). We would not be judged by whom? By God. God says, "If you will judge yourself by looking in the mirror, I will not have to judge you."

The third aspect of the laver is water, which is the Word of God as a cleansing agent.

> *Christ also loved the church and gave Himself for her, that He might sanctify and cleanse her with the washing of water by the word, that He might present her to Himself a glorious church.*
>
> (Ephesians 5:25–27)

The passage speaks of the cross where Christ sacrificed Himself. Here is the washing of water by the Word whereby He cleanses and sanctifies that which He has first redeemed by His blood. Bear this in mind: Christ redeemed the church by His blood so that He might thereafter cleanse and sanctify it with the washing of the water of the Word of God. Sanctification, holiness, and the fulfillment of God's will depend upon the blood of the cross and the water of the Word. Those who came to the brazen altar but did not wash in the laver were subject to death. You may be redeemed through your faith in Christ's death on the cross, but if you do not wash in the water of the Word, you cannot be sanctified. Jesus is coming for a church that has been made holy and glorious by the washing of water by the Word. That much is very clear. Any believer who does not study the Word and submit to the Word and obey the Word and live by the Word cannot expect to be ready for the coming of Christ.

> *This is He who came by water and blood – Jesus Christ; not only by water, but by water and blood. And it is the Spirit who bears witness, because the Spirit is truth.* (1 John 5:6)

Jesus came by water as the Great Teacher. But He is also the Redeemer who had to shed His blood. Without the shedding of blood, there is no remission of sins and no redemption. (See Hebrews 9:22.) He shed His blood so that He might thereafter cleanse and sanctify with the washing of water by the Word. He came by the water and by the blood.

– 5 –

Your Soul: An Emotional Approach to Worship

We continue on our way into the holiest. Under the old covenant, God gave Moses an earthly pattern of heavenly realities and truth. But it is only through the new covenant in Jesus Christ that we can enter into the actual heavenly realities of what was disclosed only in shadow under the old covenant.

Now we are going to go from the outer court of the temple into the Holy Place. Related to the areas of man's personality, we are moving out of the realm of the body, or the physical, and into the realm of the soul, or the emotional. Or, related to the life of Christ, we are moving out of the area of Jesus in the days when He walked the earth to that revelation of Jesus after death, through resurrection, which is only given by the inspired Scriptures.

*And He died for all, that those who live should live
no longer for themselves, but for Him who died for
them and rose again. Therefore, from now on, we
regard no one according to the flesh. Even though
we have known Christ according to the flesh …*

(2 Corinthians 5:15–16)

We are speaking now about the fact that Jesus not
merely died, but He also rose. We move out of the outer
area of physical knowledge and into the area where
revelation is imparted by the Holy Spirit.

THE FIRST VEIL

Leaving the outer court, we must first pass through the
first veil or curtain. I believe this represents Christ's
resurrection. When we pass through that veil, we pass
into an area that has been opened to us by the resurrection of Jesus from the dead. It typifies, in a sense, our
identification with Christ in resurrection.

*If then you were raised with Christ, seek those things
which are above, where Christ is, sitting at the right
hand of God.* (Colossians 3:1)

We died with Christ, but Scripture says we have also
been raised with Him.

THE HOLY PLACE

Within this first Holy Place there were three main
objects: the table of bread, the lampstand, and the

golden altar of incense. I believe that these typify the corresponding functions of our soul.

The Showbread

The table of bread, or showbread, corresponds to the human will. In Scripture, bread is symbolic of strength, and the strength of the soul is not in its intellect nor in its emotions, but in its will. You can have a brilliant intellect or be highly emotional, yet remain very weak. When I preach, I am not seeking to reach people's emotions. I am seeking to reach and change their wills. It is comparatively easy to get people emotionally stirred up, but it is totally ineffective if we don't change their wills. That has to be our aim. So the showbread on the table is symbolic of the human will.

> *Referring to the Psalms, there is a key verse in the very area we are dealing with: He causes the grass to grow for the cattle, and vegetation for the service of man, that he may bring forth food from the earth, and wine that makes glad the heart of man, oil to make his face shine, and bread which strengthens man's heart.* (Psalm 104:14–15)

Here we have God's provision for the three areas of man's soul. The wine is the emotions. The oil is intellect – notice the word *shine*, which speaks of light. And the bread speaks of the will. God's provision is summed up in these three things: the grain, the wine, and the oil.

In Joel 1, God's people, who have abandoned Him, are destitute of all three items and without his presence. In Joel 2, where God said He would pour out His spirit, He also said, *"Behold, I will send you grain and new wine and oil, and you will be satisfied by them"* (Joel 2:19). Grain is the strength of the will and the Word of God. Oil is the illumination of the Holy Spirit. And wine is the joy of the Lord. You are living an impoverished life if you don't have all three. But God will be sure to provide them if we will turn to Him.

It is Christ Himself who sets the pattern for the will.

> *Therefore, when He came into the world, He said: "Sacrifice and offering You did not desire, but a body You have prepared for Me. In burnt offerings and sacrifices for sin You had no pleasure. Then I said, 'Behold, I have come; in the volume of the book it is written of Me; to do Your will, O God.'"*
>
> (Hebrews 10:5–7)

Christ's body was prepared for one purpose: to do God's will. Likewise, there is only one reason we have bodies: to do God's will. Everything else is secondary. Jesus Himself said,

> *I can of Myself do nothing. As I hear, I judge; and My judgment is righteous, because I do not seek My own will but the will of the Father who sent Me.*
>
> (John 5:30)

That is a very important principle. You can judge justly – your discernment will be correct – when you are not seeking your own will. When you are seeking the Father's will, you will not be deceived. You will have perception, you will have discernment, and you will have judgment. But when you begin to want your own will, then you will go astray.

There is a passage in Matthew where we see the final confirmation of this point: *"Let this cup pass from Me; nevertheless, not as I will, but as You will"* (Matthew 26:39). Here is the picture of Jesus surrendering His will at every point to the Father. Likewise, it is through the surrendering of your will that you will discover the perfect will of God.

What gave Jesus strength was doing the will of God. This can be seen in His conversation with His disciples after meeting the Samaritan woman at the well:

> *In the meantime His disciples urged Him, saying, "Rabbi, eat." But He said to them, "I have food to eat of which you do not know." Therefore the disciples said to one another, "Has anyone brought Him anything to eat?" Jesus said to them, "My food is to do the will of Him who sent Me, and to finish His work."* (John 4:31–34)

Jesus was physically weak when He sat at the well, but when He witnessed to the woman and fulfilled God's will, it gave Him actual physical strength. He no longer felt an immediate need to eat. The same is true for us. It is doing the will of God that gives us strength. It is setting our will to do God's will that gives our souls strength and purpose.

The word *showbread* is not a literal translation. It is actually "the bread of the face." Whose face? This was the bread that was always before the face of God. In Numbers, it is called "continual" bread. (See Numbers 4:7 NASB.) This was the bread that was continually before God's face day and night, seven days a week. I cannot think of anything that has more deeply affected me than the understanding that my will is like loaves of bread on a table displayed before God day and night, twenty-four hours a day. God demands to inspect my will. There were precisely twelve loaves on the table – if there is one loaf missing or out of place, He wants to know why.

I promise you that if you can understand this point, you will be spared many disasters and heartaches. It is your will that you have to guard. It is your will where everything really begins in your dealings with God.

The provision for the showbread is found in Leviticus:

> *And you shall take fine flour and bake twelve cakes with it. Two-tenths of an ephah shall be in each cake. You shall set them in two rows, six in a row, on the pure gold table before the LORD. And you shall put pure frankincense on each row, that it may be on*

> *the bread for a memorial, an offering made by fire*
> *to the LORD. Every Sabbath he shall set it in order*
> *before the LORD continually, being taken from the*
> *children of Israel by an everlasting covenant. And*
> *it shall be for Aaron and his sons.*
>
> (Leviticus 24:5–9)

Here I see eight successive features in which the showbread typifies the kind of will God is looking for. First, to make the showbread, the grain has to be ground very fine. *"Bread corn is bruised"* (Isaiah 28:28 KJV). This is God, dealing with man's will in which a continual bruising of the will occurs. Your will is acceptable when it is as smooth and as fine as that flour. Until it is, God will go on bruising, bruising, bruising.

Second, to make the loaf, it must be molded. Your will must be conformed to the revealed will of God in the Scriptures. And the pattern used for the molding is Jesus. Third, after it has been molded, it has to be baked in the heat of the fire. The heat represents testing. You say, "All right, God, I want to do Your will." Then everything goes against you. Five hardships hit you in one day. Do you change your mind because you cannot stand the fire? Do not think it strange that the fire is all around you. That is the baking of the bread.

Fourth, the bread has to be ordered. There have to be twelve loaves, in two rows of six. You don't have seven in one row and five in another. This is where many Christians, charismatics in particular, can get sloppy. Without discipline, you cannot be a disciple. If you don't think it matters that you have five loaves in one row and seven in another, you do not think like God. God says six loaves in each row, opposite of one another. Not haphazard; not askew. If your will is like that, your desk, your office, and your kitchen will be like that. If you have trouble keeping order in your life, check the showbread.

Fifth, the bread must be covered by frankincense, which always signifies a type of worship in Scripture. Our response cannot be, "Well, God, if You insist, I will do it." It must be, "Thank You, Lord. I am glad to do Your will. I bow my head in submission and worship. Your will be done, Lord." On earth, as it is in heaven; that is the standard.

Sixth, as already mentioned, the bread has to be continually displayed before the face of God day and night. God says, "I want to see where the bread is."

Seventh, a double protective crown surrounds it. (See Exodus 37:10–12.) So precious was the bread that one protective crown around the top of the table was not enough. They put a border with another crown so that if any little crumbs got outside the first crown, they were still protected from falling to the earth by the second crown. Similarly, there is a double crown around your will. What is the double crown? It is to watch and pray.

Watch therefore, and pray always [twenty-four hours a day] that you may be counted worthy to escape all these things. (Luke 21:36)

You must live in such a way that it would be unrighteous of God to bring the judgment that is coming upon the ungodly upon you. Watch and pray so that you may be counted worthy to escape. *"Watch and pray.... The spirit indeed is willing, but the flesh is weak"* (Matthew 26:41). Jesus said, "You said you'd follow Me all the way, but if you do not watch and pray you will be caught off guard." Sure enough, that is what happened to the disciples. That is our double protective guard to keep the showbread in place – watch and pray.

The eighth and final feature of the bread is that it has to be put there fresh. You must regularly rededicate your will to God. Smith Wigglesworth said, "Every new revelation demands a new dedication." I agree with that. Every time God shows you a new truth, a new assignment, it demands that the showbread be put on the table afresh.

In the outer court, it was what God has done for us. But when we enter the Holy Place, it is about our response to God. It begins with the will. To me, it is very clear. As I walk along the street or participate in some daily activity, I think to myself, *Is the showbread there? Is every loaf in place? Is there anything in me that's not submitted to the will of God?* I do not mean resigned to God's will; I mean positively delighting to do His will.

The Lampstand

The next item of furniture within the Holy Place is the seven-branched candlestick, which I liken to the intellect – the source of light. The lampstand was illuminated by olive oil. This represents the human intellect as illuminated by the Holy Spirit.

The lampstand and the cherubim on the ark of the covenant within the Holy of Holies were both made of beaten gold. Everything else in the tabernacle was made of pure gold. Pure gold is divine in nature; beaten gold is of divine workmanship. Similarly, just as the cherubim were created beings, the mind is also a creation of God. Furthermore, beaten gold suggests a process of shaping, hammering, and forming something into a certain pattern. I believe it represents two facets of our intellect: study and discipline. For the lampstand of your intellect to be what God intends, it has to be beaten or shaped.

> *Casting down arguments and every high thing that exalts itself against the knowledge of God, bringing every thought into captivity to the obedience of Christ.*　　　　　(2 Corinthians 10:5)

Here is a verse that obviously applies to the area of the mind. The suggestion is that, when left to our own nature, our thoughts are in opposition to God. *"The carnal mind is enmity against God"* (Romans 8:7). Every thought of that enemy (the carnal mind) has to be brought into captivity to the obedience of Christ. That process is the hammering out of the golden lampstand.

Do you know how to tell when your mind is in the captivity of Christ? When everything you think is in line with Scripture.

As someone trained in philosophy before I came to Christ, I have probably had more problems with my mind than the average Christian. God has shown me that this was the weak area of my life. He showed me that I needed protection for my mind and gave me a helmet of hope. (See 1 Thessalonians 5:8.) He showed me that the world is alienated from God in the attitude of its mind. One of the great ministries of the gospel is bringing people's minds into captivity to the obedience of Christ. But God revealed to me that I had to start with my own mind. I have certainly not arrived, but I have a very different mind from the one I had when I was a young man. I have deliberately hammered away at the lampstand to bring every thought into captivity. This is the process every believer is to go through.

In Psalms, we see that light is related to understanding:

> *The entrance of Your words gives light; it gives understanding to the simple.* (Psalm 119:130)

And then, in Ephesians, we see that this understanding is a spiritual process. *"Be renewed in the spirit of your mind"* (Ephesians 4:23). The word *"renewed"* is in the continuing present tense, suggesting that the mind is continually and progressively renewed. It is not a one-time event.

Understanding comes from yielding up your mind to the Holy Spirit. As the Holy Spirit takes over your mind, He will bring it into line with the Book He wrote – the Bible. When the Holy Spirit captivates your mind, your mind agrees with Scripture in every point. But it is a process.

Just as Jesus sets the pattern for the will, we see that He does the same for the mind:

> *Let this mind be in you which was also in Christ Jesus.*　　　　　　　　(Philippians 2:5)

Learn to think the way Jesus thought. As the passage continues, you will see that the key word is *humility*:

> *Who, being in the form of God, did not consider it robbery to be equal with God.*　(Philippians 2:6)

Jesus humbled Himself to the point of death on the cross. That is the mind that was in Jesus. The mind must undergo its crucifixion. That is the process of bringing your proud, stubborn mind into captivity, to obedience, to humility, and to death on the cross. The crucified

mind doesn't argue with God. It does not say, "But...."
It says, "Amen."

The illumination of the intellect depends upon the
yielding of the will. You cannot have your intellect illuminated until you yield your will. The illuminated intellect
always reveals the condition of the will. After all, in the
temple, the candlestick was over the table of showbread.

If your will gets out of order, your illuminated intellect will reveal it, but will also resent it. Then, you will
go into darkness. Instead of getting true revelation,
you will get false revelation. Jesus said, *"If therefore the
light that is in you is darkness, how great is that darkness!"*
(Matthew 6:23).

The place of revelation, the Holy of Holies where we
are headed, is the holiest of all. To receive true revelation,
you must be rightly related to the holiest of all. If you
are not in right relationship to the source of revelation,
you will only receive false revelation. This is the order of
divine revelation and direction from God for the believer.
It is God's Spirit that controls and operates in the believer's spirit, which controls the believer's soul, and which
controls the believer's body. So, as with everything, the
initiative, the source of origin, is with God, and it all
depends on the will being fully yielded to God.

The Golden Altar of Incense

The final item within the Holy Place, the golden altar
of incense, was the tallest item in the room. It was two

cubits high, while everything else was one and a half cubits high. It had horns on top at each corner of the altar. Between the horns, a fire burned, but no sacrificial animal was burned in this flame. The only item placed in this fire was the special incense, created from a certain formula that was unlawful to ever be copied or used in any other situation but on that one golden altar. In other words, the altar of incense represents the place of worship in the life of the believer. There is a worship we give to God that we must never offer to any other. Don't become a worshiper of preachers, because that is misusing the incense that only belongs on the altar that leads to the presence of God.

We can identify eight features of the golden altar of incense. Remember, we are still in the area that relates to the soul of man. God first deals with the will (the showbread), then with the intellect (the lampstand), and then He is prepared to turn your emotions loose. Some people are afraid of emotions in religion. But that isn't really logical since emotions are such an essential part of man. Certainly, it is possible for the emotions to become out of control and disorderly, but this particular pattern that we are following shows us how we might bring our emotions back under control.

God desires that we be in control of our emotions, and not let our emotions control us. It is the will that determines control. I can dance and celebrate and turn loose like most people. But it isn't my emotions that make me do it; it is my will. I cannot allow my emotions to dictate to me. That is not to say that I appear unemotional. I have emotions, but they must come in their right place.

I believe you can have full reign of your emotions when your will and your intellect have been dealt with. But if you do it the other way around, then you are the slave of your emotions.

Thus, the first feature of the altar is that it was four sided and square; it was equal in every dimension. This signifies that your emotions must be balanced, not given to one type of emotion or another.

Second, as the table of showbread was protected with two crowns, the golden altar of incense was protected by one. What is the crown that protects the emotions? It is nothing else but self-control. Remember, you are in charge of your emotions. Never let them take charge of you.

Third, the fire symbolizes intensity, purity, and the passion of the soul. Far from wanting us to be unemotional, God wants us to be passionate people. But it is a controlled, purified, and directed passion.

Kate Booth Clibborn, the daughter of William Booth, once said, "Jesus loves us passionately, and He wants to be loved passionately." He certainly does. Passion is part of holiness, but it has to be in the right relationship and under the right control. The fourth aspect of the golden altar was the incense, which spoke of devotion made fragrant by the test of fire. Frankincense is a black, unattractive lump until you put it on the fire. Then it becomes wonderfully fragrant. Honey, on the other hand, is sweet and pleasant until you put it on the fire. Then it becomes a sticky, black mess. And God said that He didn't want any honey on the offerings of the Lord made by fire. (See Leviticus 2:11.) No sweet talk or nice phrases if it won't stand the test of fire.

Fifth was the smoke rising up. Beautiful and fragrant, the white smoke is adoration expressed in praise and worship.

Sixth, the horns of the altar had to be purified with the blood of the propitiatory sacrifice every year on the Day of Atonement. In other words, our worship must always acknowledge that we only have access by the blood of Jesus. If we ever offer worship that isn't through the blood of Jesus, it is totally unacceptable to God. The altar had to be sanctified by the blood. It was the tallest piece of furniture. The horns brought it up to the approximate height of the cherubim on the mercy seat. Thus, when we launch out in praise and adoration and worship, we are rising up like the smoke of the incense to the highest spiritual levels.

And finally, the altar is the transition from the soul to the spirit, from the holy to the most holy. There is no other appointed way but the way of praise, adoration, and worship.

Thus, we approach that inner place of holiness with

our attitude in line – our will, intellect, and emotion in accordance with God's requirements. Now, we are ready to enter into the very presence of God and discover true worship.

– 6 –

Your Spirit: The Way into the Holiest

We have traveled through the tabernacle, this triune building representing the triune nature of man. We have likened the three areas of the tabernacle to the three areas of human personality: the outer court, the body; the Holy Place, the soul; and now the Holy of Holies, representing man's spirit.

THE SECOND VEIL

As we leave the Holy Place, we pass through a second veil. Only on the Day of Atonement, on this one day a year, was a priest allowed to go beyond the second veil. He went with the blood from the brazen altar and with a censer filled with burning coals of fire and incense from the golden altar of incense. This is because the way to the holiest is with the blood of the everlasting sacrifice, and with the incense of worship and adoration. Without worship, we have no access beyond the Holy Place. Until we learn true worship, we are confined in the realm of the soul. The only way out is through worship sanctified by the blood. I see this veil as representing Christ's ascension.

> *But God...made us alive together with Christ (by grace you have been saved), and raised us up together, and made us sit together in the heavenly places in Christ Jesus.*   (Ephesians 2:4–6)

Not merely are we raised from the dead with Him, but Scripture says we have also been raised up to sit with Him in the heavenly places. The first veil typifies resurrection from the dead. This second veil typifies the ascension that takes us up into the heavenlies and seats us positionally on the throne with Christ.

THE HOLY OF HOLIES

You will remember that within the Holy of Holies there was no light except for the manifest, visible, personal presence of God – the *shechinah* glory. That is where worship takes place. We don't need any other source of illumination when we are in the presence of God. Here we experience the privilege of direct person-to-Person, spirit-to-Spirit relationship with God.

Within the Holy of Holies were two items of furniture that occupied the same space. First, there was the ark of the covenant. And above the ark was the mercy seat with cherubim, one on each end.

The three activities of the spirit – worship, fellowship, and revelation – have meaning only in relation to God Himself. Man's spirit is dead unless it is united with God. Your body and soul can operate without direct relationship with God, but the spirit only comes alive in contact with the Creator. When your spirit is separated from God, it is dead, darkened, and blind. So, all activities of the spirit have meaning only in relation to God Himself.

THE ARK OF THE COVENANT

The ark is Christ, revealed to the spirit. Or, Christ revealed *within* your spirit, since, in our way of interpreting the temple, the Holy of Holies represents man's spirit. An ark in the Bible is always a type of Christ. For instance, the ark of Noah typifies *you in Christ*. The ark of Moses typifies *Christ in you*. But both symbolize New Testament relationships.

The Ark of the Covenant was of acacia wood, as was all the wood in the tabernacle, and was lined both inside and out with gold. The wood typified the humanity of Jesus; gold typified His divinity. Within the ark were three items: the tablets of stone containing the Ten Commandments, the golden pot of manna, and the budded rod of Aaron – which we will examine in greater detail. Later, the tabernacle was replaced by another building, which became God's dwelling place in Israel: the temple, built by Solomon. When the ark was brought into Solomon's temple, the contents had changed:

Then the priests brought in the ark of the covenant of the LORD to its place, into the inner sanctuary of the temple, to the Most Holy Place, under the wings of the cherubim. For the cherubim spread their wings over the place of the ark, and the cherubim overshadowed the ark and its poles. And the poles extended so that the ends of the poles of the ark could be seen from the holy place, in front of the inner sanctuary; but they could not be seen from outside. And they are there to this day. Nothing was in the ark except the two tablets which Moses put there at Horeb.   (2 Chronicles 5:7–10)

The golden pot of manna and Aaron's rod that budded were taken out when the tabernacle ceased and the temple was built. I believe the tabernacle was a picture of the church in this present age: light, mobile, and impermanent. Everything had poles so that it could be carried. It could all be taken down, moved, and reassembled again. That is the church in this dispensation.

I believe the temple of Solomon is the church in the next age: established, permanent, glorified, and reigning in visible power. Now it reigns invisibly – spiritually.

Two items were taken out of the ark. First, the

golden pot of manna, which was the hidden manna – in the next age it will no longer be hidden. And Aaron's rod that budded, symbolizing God's power and authority – in the next age it will be openly displayed. But the tablets of stone always remain in the ark.

The Tablets of Stone

The two tablets of stone represent God's eternal, righteous law. There is a law in the universe that is the expression of God's own righteousness. It is as unchanging and eternal as God Himself. Psalm 40 tells us about this law in relation to Christ:

> *Then I said, "Behold, I come; in the scroll of the book it is written of me. I delight to do Your will, O my God, and Your law is within my heart."*
>
> (Psalm 40:7–8)

The tablets of stone in the ark signified Christ, with God's law within His heart, never deviating by a hair's breadth from the eternal law of God's righteousness.

God offered those tablets of stone to Israel the first time, but by the time Moses came down from the mountain after receiving them, Israel was already breaking the first commandment by idolatry. In anger, Moses cast down the tablets and they were broken. The next time Moses went up the mountain, God said, "Carve out some new tablets, and I'll write on them with My finger." But the second time, Moses was not authorized to display the tablets of stone to Israel. He was commanded to place them inside the ark. Then they were covered with the mercy seat. From then on, it was a sin punishable by death to ever lift the lid from the ark. That was the end of man trying to keep the law by his own efforts. He tried once but failed before the law ever got down from the mountain. God decided that was the end of that, and created another way. Now it was not man keeping the law, but it was Christ in man, with the law in His heart – the only way of righteousness.

The ark in you, and the law in the ark – Christ being the ark. Hebrews unfolds this truth of Christ within us having the law in His heart:

> *Because finding fault with them, He says: "Behold, the days are coming, says the LORD, when I will make a new covenant with the house of Israel and with the house of Judah; not according to the covenant that I made with their fathers in the day when I took them by the hand to lead them out of the land of Egypt."* (Hebrews 8:8–9)

That covenant was set aside because Israel broke it before it was ever finalized.

> *"For this is the covenant that I will make with the house of Israel after those days, says the LORD: I will put My laws in their mind and write them on their hearts; and I will be their God, and they shall be My people."* (Hebrews 8:10)

That is the condition of being God's people: that you have God's law, not on two tablets of stone hanging on the wall, but written in your hearts. That is what makes you God's people. Paul wrote,

> *And to the Jews I became as a Jew, ... to those who are under the law, as under the law, ... to those who are without law, as without law (not being without law toward God, but under law toward Christ).*
> (1 Corinthians 9:20–21)

Actually, that is not quite the right translation. What Paul meant was, "I am in the law in Christ because Christ is the keeper of the law for me. When Christ rules my heart, then God's law rules in my heart, through Christ in my heart. But it is not me keeping the law; it is Christ living out His lawfulness in my heart. I am totally dependent on Christ. Christ in me, the hope of glory." (See Colossians 1:27.)

The Golden Pot of Manna

Next, we come to the golden pot of manna, collected from the time when God provided sustenance for His people while they were wandering in the desert. John tells us about the manna as he quotes Jesus:

> *I am the bread of life. Your fathers ate the manna in the wilderness, and are dead. This is the bread which comes down from heaven, that one may eat of it and not die.* (John 6:48–50)

Very clearly, Christ was saying, "I am the true manna, the true bread that came down from heaven." Later, He said something tremendous:

As the living Father sent Me, and I live because of the Father, so he who feeds on Me will live because of Me. (John 6:57)

In effect, Jesus was saying, "I have life by My union with the Father. And the one who believes in Me will have life by union with Me as I have union with the Father. And in that union with Me, he will feed upon Me. I will be the hidden manna in his heart. And on that manna he will feed, day by day."

In Revelation, Jesus speaks to all believers in the church, and He gives us this promise of the hidden manna:

He who has an ear, let him hear what the Spirit says to the churches. To him who overcomes I will give some of the hidden manna to eat.
(Revelation 2:17)

That is the manna in the golden pot. We feed on Christ, the manna, by our inner spiritual communion with Him. Feeding on Him, we live by Him as He lives by His union with the Father. This is the inward spiritual union with Christ within, whereby He becomes the hidden manna in our hearts.

Aaron's Rod That Budded

The third item was the budded rod of Aaron that Moses used to perform God's miracles before Pharaoh and his sorcerers. Eventually, the leaders of the other tribes of Israel challenged Aaron's authority as high priest, and as the only one with the right to enter the Holy of Holies. God said, "We will settle this once and for all. Let the head of every tribe of Israel bring Me his rod." The rod was the symbol of authority for each tribe. Each man wrote his name on his rod. As God instructed, they put all of the rods before God and came back twenty-four hours later. When they returned, eleven of the rods were just as they had left them. But the twelfth rod had budded, bringing forth blossoms and complete almonds in just twenty-four hours. On the rod that budded was written the name *Aaron*. God had vindicated Aaron's authority. (See Numbers 17:1–10.)

Today, the name on that rod is not Aaron, but *Jesus*. By the resurrection from the dead, God vindicated the divine claim of Jesus. So the rod is divine attestation and it comes by divine revelation. When you have revelation and attestation, you have authority.

Now we have a picture of what was inside the Holy of Holies. The three items within the ark signify the following, and I believe they must be in this order: worship, fellowship, and revelation. Out of our approach in worship comes fellowship. Without worship you do not have fellowship. God will not fellowship with somebody who approaches irreverently or hastily. But when you approach with worship, you enter into fellowship. You begin to feed upon the hidden manna in the golden pot. And then out of worship and fellowship comes revelation of the mind and the will and the purpose of God. The shechinah glory illuminates this place.

THE MERCY SEAT

Now that we have dealt with the ark, we look at the mercy seat, which covered the ark. As I said before, the ark is Christ. Outside of Christ, there is no mercy, no acceptance, and no life. If you are in the ark, you are under the mercy.

Romans uses the Greek word for *mercy seat*, though it isn't translated that way in the English Scripture:

Being justified freely by His grace through the redemption that is in Christ Jesus, whom God set forth as a propitiation [here is the Greek word for mercy seat] by His blood. (Romans 3:24–25)

Christ's atonement, His sacrifice, is the mercy seat. It is the place that covers the broken law, the tablets of stone that all of us have been unable to accept or keep. Now the mercy seat becomes a throne:

Let us therefore come boldly to the throne of grace, that we may obtain mercy and find grace to help in time of need. (Hebrews 4:16)

We can go boldly to the throne of grace because God sits on the mercy seat, on Christ's atoning work that covers the broken law.

On the ark were two cherubs, two heavenly creatures, in beaten gold, kneeling at each end of the ark, their faces turned inward toward one another, their wings stretched out, with the tips meeting just over the mercy seat. Here again were represented the same three activities: worship, fellowship, and revelation. The bowed wings of the cherubim are worship. Their faces, inward toward one another, are fellowship. God said that where the wings and faces met, He would reveal His glory:

> *And the cherubim shall stretch out their wings above, covering the mercy seat with their wings, and they shall face one another; the faces of the cherubim shall be toward the mercy seat. You shall put the mercy seat on top of the ark, and in the ark you shall put the Testimony that I will give you. And there I will meet with you, and I will speak with you from above the mercy seat, from between the two cherubim which are on the ark of the Testimony, about everything which I will give you in commandment to the children of Israel.* (Exodus 25:20–22)

Here, Christ sits as a King and a Priest upon His throne. I believe the life inside the ark must precede the life upon the throne. It is the hidden life in the ark that gives you access to the throne. There has to be the inner life of worship, or bowing down, before the eternal law. If you don't submit in prostration before the law of God, you have no access. You have to learn to feed upon the hidden manna. You have to have the rod that buds supernaturally with divine revelation.

When we come into the ark, we can step up on the mercy seat and sit on the throne. Jesus wants to share His throne with you, but there is an appointed way, step by step by step. I don't believe you can bypass any of these stages. There is only one way into the holiest. It is like a map; it is sketched out so plainly that an intelligent child of ten can easily understand once God reveals it.

Here we have what I would call the "end product" of entering the Holy of Holies. There is worship, an intimate communion, and feeding on God. There is revelation, imparting God's authority. And there is God's eternal law of righteousness stamped upon our consciences. This is the destination of the progression into worship. We start in the outer court with the bronze altar symbolizing Christ's death. We pass through the first veil of Christ's resurrection into the Holy Place where we give God our will, intellect, and emotions. And then we are brought through the second veil, symbolizing Christ's ascension, and into the immediate presence of God.

Then, we have entered into worship. Worship is

not essentially an utterance; it is an attitude. It is not primarily praise, although they can be blended together. Worship is the attitude with which you approach. Worship relates to the tablets of stone within the tabernacle. It is total submission to the righteous law of God that doesn't change, doesn't bend, and doesn't deviate. It is complete reverence in approaching God.

As you would proceed through the tabernacle, each area would get progressively smaller and smaller the closer you came to God. Finally, in the Holy of Holies, you would be in a perfect cube – ten cubits long, ten cubits wide, and ten cubits high. There was really nothing to attract you there but God, and that is the way He planned it. There is something within us that grows scared the farther we go in this approach. Most of us come to God for things. We want blessings, we want power, or we want healing. God wants us to come simply for Him. Thus, we don't come into this place until we come to God for God's sake. We approach God as God. We worship; we bow before Him. We feed upon Him; we enjoy Him. Then comes revelation.

– 7 –

Four Blessings of the New Covenant

It is my firm opinion that the epistle of Hebrews doesn't make any sense if you are not familiar with the tabernacle because the entire letter is based on the tabernacle and on the priesthood. I have heard it said that Leviticus is the Hebrews of the Old Testament or that Hebrews is the Leviticus of the New Testament, whichever way you would like to word it. In Hebrews 10 we see a clear application of what we have been learning:

> *Therefore, brethren, having boldness to enter the Holiest by the blood of Jesus, by a new and living way which He consecrated for us, through the veil, that is, His flesh, and having a High Priest over the house of God, let us draw near with a true heart in full assurance of faith, having our hearts sprinkled*

> *from an evil conscience and our bodies washed with*
> *pure water.*   (Hebrews 10:19–22)

These verses name four great blessings of the new covenant and the four chief requirements of the true worshiper. In this chapter, I will elaborate on the four blessings that are listed.

THE HOLY OF HOLIES OPENED UP

What an incredible privilege! It staggers my powers of expression that we have this direct access into the immediate presence of almighty God. The barrier to this access is man's sinful, fleshly nature. But this was dealt with on the cross, as it states in Romans:

> *For what the law could not do in that it was weak*
> *through the flesh, God did by sending His own Son*
> *in the likeness of sinful flesh, on account of sin: He*
> *condemned sin in the flesh.*
>
> (Romans 8:3)

The law could not do it because there was not anything wrong with the law. Paul said that the law is holy and just and good. (See Romans 7:12.) Every commandment of the law was right. Still, I could look at those tablets of stone and all the other writings of the law and say, "I'll do it," but there is something in me that says, "Oh no, you won't. In fact, the harder you try to do it, the worse you will fail." Paul stated it this way:

> *For what I am doing, I do not understand. For what I will to do, that I do not practice; but what I hate, that I do. If, then, I do what I will not to do, I agree with the law that it is good. But now, it is no longer I who do it, but sin that dwells in me....I find then a law, that evil is present with me, the one who wills to do good.* (Romans 7:15–17, 21)

The moment I try to keep the law, my carnal, rebellious nature asserts itself, and the harder I try to be good, the worse I am. I discovered this at age fifteen when I was confirmed in the Anglican Church. I really decided that it was time for me to be a lot better than I had been for a long while. I said, "This is it. I'll be confirmed, brush my teeth, go to communion, and I'll be good." I was never so bad as immediately after that confirmation.

The problem is self-confidence. *"Cursed is the man who trusts in man and makes flesh his strength, whose heart departs from the LORD"* (Jeremiah 17:5). When you say, "There is the law; I am doing it," you are putting confidence in yourself and you come under a curse. *"Cursed is the one who does not confirm all the words of this law"* (Deuteronomy 27:26). If you are going to be under the law, you have to do all the law, all the time. If you can't do that, it is of no avail. If you break one point of the law once, you are a lawbreaker forever. It's either all or nothing.

I recognize the law is good. There is something in me that says, "That's right; that's the way I should be living." *"For I delight in the law of God according to the inward man"* (Romans 7:22). But there is something else in me – a rebel.

> *But I see another law in my members, warring against the law of my mind, and bringing me into captivity to the law of sin which is in my members.*
> (Romans 7:23)

The word *captivity* means "prisoner of war." Paul was saying, "I set out to fight for God and I end up on the wrong side, fighting against Him. I am a prisoner of war. I do not do it deliberately; it is something that takes me captive. I cannot help it."

> *O wretched man that I am! Who will deliver me from this body of death?... So then, with the mind I myself serve the law of God, but with the flesh the law of sin.* (Romans 7:24–25)

That is a poor translation. A better one would be: "Left to myself, I can serve the law of God with my mind, but with my fleshly nature I am a slave of the law of sin and I cannot change it." So, what is the remedy? For what the law could not do.... (Romans 8:3)

The law couldn't change my nature. It told me *what* to do, but it couldn't give me the power to do it.

For what the law could not do in that it was weak
through the flesh, God did by sending His own Son
in the likeness of sinful flesh, on account of sin: He
condemned sin in the flesh. (Romans 8:3)

He condemned sin in whose flesh? In the flesh of Jesus. God dealt with sin in the body of Jesus. His body became the sin offering. That is where sin was dealt with, once and forever. When we appreciate that, we are free from the bondage and guilt of sin.

So, going back to the passage in Hebrews, we read:

By a new and living way which He consecrated for
us, through the veil, that is, His flesh.
(Hebrews 10:20)

Our fleshly nature is the veil, crucified in the body of Jesus. We cannot pass through that veil to come near to God; the veil has to be taken away. The fleshly nature has to be dealt with. It was dealt with in the body of Christ. When His flesh was torn on the cross for our sins, the veil was torn as well.

The temple was built in the same pattern, the triune structure, as the tabernacle: the outer court, the Holy Place, and the Holy of Holies. The temple was simply more substantial and permanent. In accordance with divine ordinance, the Holy of Holies was separated by this tremendously glorious, thick, impenetrable curtain.

But when Jesus died on the cross, just outside the city of Jerusalem, something happened to the curtain in the Holy of Holies at that precise moment:

> *And Jesus cried out again with a loud voice, and yielded up His spirit. Then, behold, the veil of the temple was torn in two from top to bottom.*
> (Matthew 27:50–51)

Let there be no doubt about where the initiative came from. It came from God, and not from man. The curtain was torn from the top to the bottom. The way was opened into the Holiest through the death of Jesus because in His flesh on the cross, God condemned and put away sin. Now, the Holy of Holies was opened up for us.

BOLDNESS IN THE BLOOD OF JESUS

We refer back to Hebrews 10 for the second blessing of the new covenant:

> *Therefore, brethren, having boldness to enter the Holiest by the blood of Jesus, by a new and living way.* (Hebrews 10:19–20)

The word *boldness* is not primarily subjective, but objective. In other words, it is not that I have an emotional boldness; it is that I have a legal boldness that comes from having an absolute, indisputable right of access. Whether or not I feel bold is secondary. This is important to understand. The word *boldness* here is somewhat misleading. It is more of an unquestionable right of access through the blood of Jesus.

In Leviticus, we have the old covenant ceremonies for the appointed day on which the high priest was allowed to enter the Holy of Holies – once a year, on the Day of Atonement. Today the Jews call it Yom Kippur, the day of covering – still a day of fasting and mourning for Orthodox Jews. The entire chapter is another tremendous presentation of the truth of entry into the holiest, but I want to deal specifically with the blood of the sin offering.

> *And Aaron [the high priest] shall bring the bull of the sin offering, which is for himself, and make atonement for himself and for his house, and shall kill the bull as the sin offering which is for himself. Then he shall take a censer full of burning coals of fire from the altar before the LORD, with his hands full of sweet incense beaten fine, and bring it inside the veil.* (Leviticus 16:11–12)

Notice that it is the blood from the altar and the incense from the altar that must be united for access through the veil.

And he shall put the incense on the fire before the LORD, that the cloud of incense may cover the mercy seat that is on the Testimony, lest he die.

(Leviticus 16:13)

This was no empty religious ceremony. This was life or death – for the priest and for the whole nation. If at any time the priest was not accepted, the entire nation lost its standing before God. He was their representative.

He shall take some of the blood of the bull and sprinkle it with his finger on the mercy seat on the east side; and before the mercy seat he shall sprinkle some of the blood with his finger seven times.

(Leviticus 16:14)

The number seven tells us that it is through the Holy Spirit. In the same way, Jesus *"through the eternal Spirit offered Himself without spot to God"* (Hebrews 9:14). The blood was sprinkled on and before the mercy seat. Actually, there was a train of blood all the way through the tabernacle. Without blood, there is no access. We see the parallel in the New Testament. The atonement of Jesus was not terminated on earth; it was consummated in heaven. This is clearly stated in Hebrews:

This hope we have as an anchor of the soul, both sure and steadfast, and which enters the Presence behind the veil, where the forerunner has entered for us, even Jesus. (Hebrews 6:19–20)

Here, we are not talking about the earthly tabernacle; we are talking about the tabernacle in heaven. Jesus has entered within the veil. A forerunner is a representative, someone who says, "There are others coming after me. From now on, the way is open for them to follow me." Jesus is our forerunner. He has entered within the veil.

Then, further on in Hebrews, the Scripture says,

> *But Christ came as High Priest of the good things*
> *to come…*   (Hebrews 9:11)

A better translation is "good things that have actually been accomplished." In other words, in contrast to the law, which had only types and shadows and promises and patterns, this is real – it really happened.

> *But Christ came as High Priest of the good things to*
> *come, with the greater and more perfect tabernacle*
> *not made with hands, that is, not of this creation.*
> *Not with the blood of goats and calves, but with His*
> *own blood He entered the Most Holy Place once for*
> *all, having obtained eternal redemption.*(Hebrews
> 9:11–12)

Jesus took His blood with Him into the Holiest.

> *Therefore it was necessary that the copies of the*
> *things in the heavens should be purified with these,*
> *but the heavenly things themselves with better sac-*
> *rifices than these.*   (Hebrews 9:23)

The heavenly things had to be purified, but not with the blood of bulls and goats.

> *For Christ has not entered the holy places made with hands, which are copies of the true, but into heaven itself, now to appear in the presence of God for us.* (Hebrews 9:24)

How did Christ enter into the Holiest? With His own blood. And this becomes even clearer when we turn to the twelfth chapter of Hebrews:

> *But you have come to Mount Zion and to the city of the living God, the heavenly Jerusalem....* (Hebrews 12:22)

This is not the earthly Jerusalem. We have come, not physically, but by the Spirit.

> *...to an innumerable company of angels, to the general assembly and church of the firstborn who are registered in heaven, to God the Judge of all, to the spirits of just men made perfect.* (Hebrews 12:22–23)

That is you and me. Our headquarters is in heaven. Are you enrolled in heaven in the Lamb's Book of Life, or are you just on the roll of the church? It is all right to be on the roll of the church, but it is not sufficient.

*...to Jesus the Mediator of the new covenant, and
to the blood of sprinkling that speaks better things
than that of Abel.* (Hebrews 12:24)

Abel's blood was sprinkled on earth. What did it call
out for? Vengeance. Jesus' blood is sprinkled in heaven.
What does it call out for? Mercy. If you can believe that
the blood of Jesus is always speaking on your behalf in
the very presence of God, this is a tremendous truth. If
it weren't, you would never get to heaven. God, as Judge,
would never bring you there. Even Jesus did not enter
heaven without His blood. It is the only access; through
the blood of Jesus sprinkled in heaven.

THE NEW AND LIVING WAY

The third of the great blessings of the new covenant is
the new and living way – which is Jesus. Jesus becomes
the way; He becomes the truth; He becomes the life;
but He is the way all the way through. The way that Jesus
went in is the way that we go; there is no other way. It
is a way of self-denial, obedience, sacrifice, and death.
That is the new and living way.

*For to this you were called, because Christ also suf-
fered for us, leaving us an example, that you should
follow His steps.* (1 Peter 2:21)

The steps of Jesus are the new and living way. What
is the first step when you want to follow Jesus?

Then Jesus said to His disciples, "If anyone desires to come after Me, let him deny himself."

(Matthew 16:24)

Self-denial. That doesn't mean just giving up radishes for Lent! That's fine, but it isn't self-denial. Self-denial is saying no to the ego. When self says, "I want," self-denial is the ability to say, "No." When self says, "I think," self-denial says, "No." What you think is not the least bit important. If what you think still matters, you have not denied yourself. Denying yourself is saying no to that old goat inside you.

Likewise, self-denial is not giving up the vile sin. That may be needed, but self-denial is denying the ego, the "I" that asserts itself and makes itself important, demanding that the world center around itself: what I want, what I think, and what I feel. It is all irrelevant as far as God is concerned.

The first step in actually following Jesus is saying no to all that. If any man will take up his cross, let him deny himself. In Matthew 26, we have the climax for self-denial:

He went a little farther and fell on His face, and prayed, saying, "O My Father, if it is possible, let this cup pass from Me; nevertheless, not as I will, but as You will." … Again, a second time, He went away and prayed, saying, "O My Father, if this cup cannot pass away from Me unless I drink it, Your will be done." (Matthew 26:39, 42)

Every new move in God begins with the repetition of, *"Not as I will, but as You will."* Jesus didn't just renounce His will once. Every time He was confronted with the choice between His will and the Father's will, He repeated the renunciation, *"Not as I will, but as You will."* That is the new and living way.

The wonderful thing about this is that when you set your heart on following God, you rejoice. Though it sounds hard, it fills you with joy. But if your heart isn't set on following God, then all you can see is the unpleasantness of it.

> *For it was fitting for Him, for whom are all things and by whom are all things, in bringing many sons to glory, to make the captain of their salvation perfect through sufferings.* (Hebrews 2:10)

Jesus was made perfect through suffering. He is our leader. We are made perfect in the same way that He was made perfect – through the sufferings that come from obedience. From saying, *"Not as I will, but as You will"* (Matthew 26:39). Not from the suffering that comes from disobedience. That type of suffering does not purify you, refine you, or make you perfect.

> *For both He who sanctifies and those who are being sanctified are all of one.* (Hebrews 2:11)

"He who sanctifies" is Jesus. *"Those who are being sanctified"* are you and I. And the *"one"* of whom we all

come – Jesus and you and I – is the Father. So we are sanctified by the Father in the way that Jesus was made perfect. It is the Jesus way that leads to sanctification, holiness, and perfection. That is the way.

> *[Jesus], in the days of His flesh, when He had offered up prayers and supplications, with vehement cries and tears to Him who was able to save Him from death, and was heard because of His godly fear....*
> (Hebrews 5:7)

The *New English Bible* says, *"Because of His humble submission He was heard."* His prayer was heard. That is the spirit of access to God. Jesus is the perfect pattern. He was heard because He feared. This is the root answer as to why prayers are not answered. I can give you half a dozen other reasons, but God has showed me that this is the root. You can teach people all the principles of getting their prayers answered, but if their attitude is wrong, the principles don't work. The attitude comes first. He was heard because of His humble submission.

> *...though He was a Son, yet He learned obedience by the things which He suffered.*
> (Hebrews 5:8)

He found out what it was to obey by suffering as a consequence of obeying.

And having been perfected, He became the author
of eternal salvation to all who obey Him.

(Hebrews 5:9)

The same way He went is the way – the new and living way.

Jesus was God, is God, and always will be God. And He became man, finally and forever. Do not forget, He is still a man. *"For there is one God and one Mediator between God and men, the Man Christ Jesus"* (1 Timothy 2:5).

When He emptied Himself, He didn't do it conditionally; He just emptied Himself. He was obedient unto death and, as it says in Philippians 2:9, *"Therefore God also has highly exalted Him."* Having emptied Himself, He had to earn His way back to that place of exaltation. *"Therefore"* indicates that His exaltation was the result of His obedience. If He had disobeyed, He would never have gotten back. So He is the perfect pattern of development, maturity, and perfection. He had to be made perfect as a man through obedience. How then will we be made perfect? Through obedience – so leave the theology to one side and just obey.

WE HAVE A GREAT HIGH PRIEST

What do we have so far? We have the Holiest opened to us. We have an objective right of access through the blood. And we have a new and living way to avail ourselves of this access. Now we have a Great High Priest waiting there for us. Who is He? Jesus. He is the High Priest in two respects.

We have such a High Priest, who is seated at the right hand of the throne of the Majesty in the heavens, a Minister of the sanctuary.

(Hebrews 8:1–2)

First of all, He is a minister of the sanctuary. Has it ever occurred to you that the high priest in Israel had to know quite a bit? He had a lot of rules to observe. He had to know how to kill the animal, what to do with the liver, the legs, the heart, the head, and the skin. He had to know on which side of the altar to sprinkle the blood. All the way through, there were a great many precise requirements that had to be complied with. Jesus is the minister of the true sanctuary. When He went in, He did everything right. He met all of God's requirements as a priest all the way through. Because He did everything right, our access is guaranteed.

Second, He is the mediator of the new covenant:

And for this reason He is the Mediator of the new covenant. (Hebrews 9:15)

He ministers the benefits of His sacrifice to you and me by the Holy Spirit. He imparts to us – He works out in us as we follow in this way – what is required in each phase of access. He is the one who makes the covenant work in you and me. Having done all the groundwork, having gone in to God, He turns around and does everything that is needed in everyone who obeys Him to make our access perfect. He mediates the covenant.

Thus, we have the four blessings of the new covenant. First, the veil is torn and the way is open. Second, we have an objective, legal, unquestionable right of access through the blood. Third, we have a living way to go in, the way that Jesus went: obedience, self-denial, sacrifice, and the death of the old man. Jesus said that whoever loses his life will find it. (See Matthew 10:39.) The Greek word used there for *life* is "soul." You have to lay down that soulish ego and say, "No." Then you will find the way inside. And fourth, we have a Great High Priest who knows exactly what needs to be done, and does it perfectly.

– 8 –

Four Requirements
of True Worshipers

Returning to the book of Hebrews, we see the four chief requirements of the true worshiper – what God expects of His worshipers if they are to avail themselves of what He has made available to them:

> *Let us draw near with a true heart in full assurance*
> *of faith, having our hearts sprinkled from an evil*
> *conscience and our bodies washed with pure water.*
> (Hebrews 10:22)

A TRUE HEART

What does a "true heart" mean? I will offer my opinion. Sincerity, honesty, loyalty, total commitment, no reservations – that is a true heart.

If I love my wife with a true heart, I love her totally. I

will not in any circumstance contemplate anything that would be disloyal to her. I think a word that we need to restore to our vocabulary is the word *loyalty*. Loyalty has become passé and out-of-date among some people today. Loyalty to your family. Loyalty to your country.

What was it that made the apostle John stand in front of the cross by Mary's side when all the other disciples had fled? Was it theology? Not for a moment. It was loyalty. What was it that got Mary Magdalene to the tomb in the early hours of the morning? Was it doctrine? No, it was loyalty. She was going to be loyal to that man even if he was nothing but a brutally mutilated corpse. There does not seem to be much loyalty among some believers today. We must be loyal to Jesus and loyal to one another. That is a true heart.

> *Behold, You desire truth in the inward parts, and in the hidden part You will make me to know wisdom. Purge me with hyssop, and I shall be clean; wash me, and I shall be whiter than snow. Make me hear joy and gladness, that the bones You have broken may rejoice. Hide Your face from my sins, and blot out all my iniquities. Create in me a clean heart, O God, and renew a steadfast spirit within me.*
>
> (Psalm 51:6–10)

The word *behold* is dramatic. David had been religious a long while, but now he had made a discovery, "*You desire truth in the inward parts, and in the hidden part You will make me to know wisdom."* I believe truth and wisdom go together. You don't know the hidden wisdom until you have truth in the inward parts. The revelation of hidden wisdom is not through the mind, but through the sincere, true, and honest heart.

When sin has had its way in your heart, it can't be patched up, repaired, or modified. It takes a creative act of God to give you a clean heart. In Psalm 139, David was talking about God's enemies and said,

> *Do I not hate them, O LORD, who hate You? And do I not loathe those who rise up against You? I hate them with perfect hatred; I count them my enemies.*
> (Psalm 139:21–22)

Is it right for a Christian to say that? Some people might say yes, and some would say no. David went to a different source:

> *Search me, O God, and know my heart; try me, and know my anxieties.* (Psalm 139:23)

David was asking God, "Is there something inside of me that is an enemy of God? See if there is something inside of me that is opposed to You." Can you invite God to do that? Do not be afraid. When it comes to confession, I tell people to remember that you are not going to confess anything to God that He does not already know. There will be no surprises. The confession is for your sake, not His.

*See if there is any wicked way in me, and lead me
in the way everlasting.* (Psalm 139:24)

Before God can lead us in this everlasting way, we
have to allow Him to search and try our hearts – to root
out any of God's enemies lurking there. Let God show
you what is in your heart and then let Him deal with it.
Lay it bare to Him.

In Isaiah, it says,

*Therefore the LORD said: "Inasmuch as these people
draw near with their mouths and honor Me with
their lips, but have removed their hearts far from
Me, and their fear toward Me is taught by the commandment of men...."* (Isaiah 29:13)

That is religion without heart. It honors God with
the lips, but its heart is far from Him. The great sin of
religious people was the one that Jesus dealt with most
severely in the Pharisees: hypocrisy. Do you know what
hypocrisy is? The word comes from the Greek word
for *actor*. Religion is simply putting on an act. Ancient
drama utilized several types of masks. When an actor
portrayed different parts, he would put on different
masks. Empty religion merely puts on a selection of
masks – it is a way to act while you are in church. You
will find that many religious people use even a different
tone of voice inside the church. When they pray, they
take on an artificial, false voice.

And God says He has removed from the hypocrite the ability to see the truth:

Therefore, behold, I will again do a marvelous work among this people, a marvelous work and a wonder; for the wisdom of their wise men shall perish, and the understanding of their prudent men shall be hidden. (Isaiah 29:14)

God wants worshipers with a true heart, no hypocrisy, no religious acts. He wants sincere hearts, loyal and true. I have heard it said that we translate faith by obedience. I would suggest that we translate faith by loyalty – loyalty to Christ at any cost. I think you will find they work to exactly the same end.

FULLNESS OF FAITH

So the first requirement of the true worshiper is a true heart. The next condition is fullness of faith. Do you have fullness of faith? Is it an effort or a struggle? Do you have to pinch yourself and say, "Am I full of faith?" No, faith is a decision. That is why unbelief is the primary sin. What is it to have fullness of faith? Let us look at the Psalms:

Therefore all Your precepts concerning all things I consider to be right; I hate every false way.
(Psalm 119:128)

Whatever God says is right. Anything that disagrees with Him is a false way. That is not a feeling or emotion;

that is a decision. I intend to agree with what God says. When I was saved and baptized in the Holy Spirit in an army barracks, not knowing anything about New Testament doctrine, I clutched hold of one fact: the Bible was the book with the answers. It is the Book that tells me what has happened to me.

Intellectual arguments are basically an unwillingness to make a decision. If you wait until you understand the entire Bible before you will believe it, you will be waiting a long while. If you wait to understand everything about Jesus Christ before you accept Him, you will wait a long while. Faith is a decision in relation to Christ and the Scripture. I have made that decision, thank God. My mind is at rest. I have perfect inward peace.

> *Casting down arguments and every high thing that exalts itself against the knowledge of God, bringing every thought into captivity to the obedience of Christ.* (2 Corinthians 10:5)

You can do what this verse describes. Inside you, there is a mind that is trained to argue with God. By nature, it is opposed to God. *"Because the carnal mind is enmity against God"* (Romans 8:7). It is your responsibility to suppress that enemy; refuse to give him liberty to speak.

> *But let him ask in faith, with no doubting, for he who doubts is like a wave of the sea driven and*

> *tossed by the wind. For let not that man suppose*
> *that he will receive anything from the Lord; he is a*
> *double-minded man, unstable in all his ways.*
>
> (James 1:6–8)

The double-minded, unstable, undecided person gets nowhere with God. Make up your mind from now on that what God says is right. That is the fullness of faith.

But I must give you an additional warning the Lord gave me:

> *And for this reason God will send them strong delu-*
> *sion, that they should believe the lie, that they all*
> *may be condemned who did not believe the truth.*
>
> (2 Thessalonians 2:11–12)

That Scripture should take your breath away if you are not familiar with it. It is very simple. If you don't believe the truth, you will believe a lie. That was Eve's choice. God told her the truth; Satan told her a lie. She had two options. She chose the lie – that is unbelief. What is unbelief? It is believing the lie. It does not mean believing in nothing; everybody believes in something. The decision is always the same – Will I believe God, or will I believe Satan? God says if you do not believe the truth, He will see to it that you believe the lie.

Do not fool around with this. Do not believe just as much as it suits you and leave the rest. Incomplete obedience is disobedience. Incomplete belief is unbelief. You can receive the truth, or you can come under delusion. As this age closes, those are the only two options available to God's people.

HEARTS SPRINKLED FROM AN EVIL CONSCIENCE

The next requirement of the true worshiper is a heart sprinkled from an evil conscience.

Much more then, having now been justified by His blood, we shall be saved from wrath through Him.
(Romans 5:9)

Romans tells us that we are justified by the blood of Jesus. If you know my teaching, you know my definition of justified: "just-as-if-I'd" never sinned. That is how righteous the blood of Jesus makes us. There is no more guilty conscience for sin.

There is therefore now no condemnation to those who are in Christ Jesus. (Romans 8:1)

If we confess our sins, He is faithful and just to forgive us our sins and to cleanse us from all unrighteousness. (1 John 1:9)

If our heart does not condemn us, we have confidence toward God. (1 John 3:21)

On the other hand, if I am condemned in any way within my heart, I have no access to God.

If I regard iniquity in my heart, the Lord will not hear. (Psalm 66:18)

You have to make a faith stand: "All my sins are forgiven. I have confessed them all. God has forgiven them all. The blood of Jesus Christ cleanses me from all unrighteousness. I am justified – just-as-if-I'd never sinned." Do you believe that? I do. I really believe it. I do not allow my mind to insinuate any religious doubt. I believe that God is faithful and just. I believe He has forgiven me all my sins and cleansed me from all unrighteousness. I do not have to cringe in the presence of God. I do not have to whimper. I can walk upright. *"I have…made you walk upright"* (Leviticus 26:13). Hebrews goes one better than that:

"Their sins and their lawless deeds I will remember no more." (Hebrews 10:17)

God does not have a bad memory; He is a great forgetter! There is a big difference. God remembers everything that He does not decide to forget. If He decides to forget it, He does not remember it anymore.

BODIES WASHED WITH PURE WATER

Did you know that the condition of your body affects your access to God?

Let us draw near with a true heart in full assurance of faith, having our hearts sprinkled from an evil conscience and our bodies washed with pure water.

(Hebrews 10:22)

What does it mean to have your body washed with pure water? What is the pure water? The pure water is the Word of God. How does God's Word purify us?

Since you have purified your souls in obeying the truth through the Spirit.

(1 Peter 1:22)

God's Word purifies us through the Spirit. The Word, ministered by the Spirit and obeyed, purifies you.

And everyone who has this hope in Him [Jesus Christ] purifies himself, just as He is pure.

(1 John 3:3)

Obey the Word ministered to you through the Spirit, and you purify yourself. How pure must we be? Even as He is pure. There is only one standard that God has – Jesus.

For this is the will of God, your sanctification: that you should abstain from sexual immorality; that each of you should know how to possess his own vessel in sanctification and honor.

(1 Thessalonians 4:3–4)

Your body is the vessel, and the Bible says it is the will of God that you should know how to keep that vessel unsoiled – pure and holy.

Now may the God of peace Himself sanctify you completely; and may your whole spirit, soul, and body be preserved blameless at the coming of our Lord Jesus Christ. (1 Thessalonians 5:23)

Scripture says your body should be preserved blameless unto the coming of the Lord. That is complete holiness. If your body is not preserved blameless, whatever that may mean, it is not total holiness. The will of God is that you should know how to possess this vessel in sanctification and honor.

In 1 Corinthians 6, the main theme is the importance of the body. Most Christians grow up with the attitude that the body is not really that important. The Bible does not say that. Please note, it is not scriptural to belittle your body.

All things are lawful for me, but all things are not helpful. All things are lawful for me, but I will not be brought under the power of any.
(1 Corinthians 6:12)

It is all right for me to eat three ice cream sundaes, but it does not do me any good. Ice cream, cigarettes, and coffee should not be dictating to me. As Lester

Sumrall once said, "The morning I wake up and feel I cannot do without a cup of coffee is the morning I will not drink it." That is a pretty good decision to make. When you become dependent on anything, you become enslaved by it.

> *Foods for the stomach and the stomach for foods, but God will destroy both it and them.*
>
> (1 Corinthians 6:13)

Food for the stomach, and the stomach for food. But neither of them is permanent. Enjoy them while you have them; it will not be for long.

> *Now the body is not for sexual immorality but for the Lord, and the Lord for the body.*
>
> (1 Corinthians 6:13)

Most Christians would say "amen" to the first part of that verse, but what does it mean that your body is for the Lord, and the Lord for your body?

> *And God both raised up the Lord and will also raise us up by His power. Do you not know that your bodies are members of Christ?*
>
> (1 Corinthians 6:14–15)

Christ's members on earth are our physical members. That is all He has to work with.

Shall I then take the members of Christ and make them members of a harlot? Certainly not! Or do you not know that he who is joined to a harlot is one body with her? For "the two," He says, "shall become one flesh." But he who is joined to the Lord is one spirit with Him. (1 Corinthians 6:15–17)

Earlier we talked about the union of man's spirit with the Spirit of God in worship. Here again, we see the direct parallel between the relation of the prostitute and the spiritual relation to the Lord. He who is united in the love relationship with the Lord is one in spirit with Him.

Flee sexual immorality. Every sin that a man does is outside the body, but he who commits sexual immorality sins against his own body. Or do you not know that your body is the temple of the Holy Spirit who is in you, whom you have from God, and you are not your own? For you were bought at a price; therefore glorify God in your body and in your spirit, which are God's.

(1 Corinthians 6:18–20)

Sexual sins defile the body. You do not belong to yourself, and that includes your body. You are the property of God. The supreme purpose of your body is to serve as a temple for the Holy Spirit. "*The Most High does not dwell in temples made with hands*" (Acts 7:48).

You can build Him the nicest church or cathedral and He may come there when His people are there, but His dwelling place is the physical body of the redeemed believer.

> *Go therefore and make disciples of all the nations, baptizing them in the name of the Father and of the Son and of the Holy Spirit.* (Matthew 28:19)

After you commit your life to Christ, you are baptized – submersed in a cleansing, sanctifying application of water. Everything that was offered to God on the altar of blood must be washed in the water. It is not to make you physically clean but to make you holy in the true sense of being set apart to God. Peter said, *"Repent, and let every one of you be baptized"* (Acts 2:38). How many? All of you. Once you have done that, you are to present your body as a *"living sacrifice."* Paul wrote,

> *I beseech you therefore, brethren, by the mercies of God, that you present your bodies a living sacrifice…to God.* (Romans 12:1)

Your body is sanctified when it is placed on God's altar. That is how to preserve your body in sanctification and honor. Keep it on the altar. Jesus said to the Pharisees, in effect, "You fools! It is not the gift that sanctifies the altar; it is the altar that sanctifies the gift." (See Matthew 23:18–19.) If you place your body on God's altar, as long as it is in contact with the altar, it is sanctified. But if you break the contact, you have lost your sanctification.

Your body does not belong to you; it belongs to God.

Therefore do not let sin reign in your mortal body, that you should obey it in its lusts. And do not present your members as instruments of unrighteousness to sin, but present yourselves to God as being alive from the dead, and your members as instruments of righteousness to God. (Romans 6:12–13)

To summarize, you have your heart sprinkled from an evil conscience, you know your sins are forgiven, you know your heart is cleansed, and then you have your body washed with pure water – the pure water of the Word of God. You purify yourself by obeying the truth ministered to you by the Holy Spirit. The first purifying act after believing is being immersed, passing through the water, being set apart to God. After that, you lay your body, sanctified by blood and water, on the altar of God's service. You present every individual member to God as an instrument. And your body thereafter is a vessel for Him. It is the only instrument that Jesus Christ has on this earth by which to do His will at this time. Our members are the members of Christ.

– 9 –
Our Physical Attitude of Worship

There is no such thing as motionless worship. There is no such thing as worship in which our body makes no response. Worship is intensely active. I've had the privilege of being able to read the Bible in both the Hebrew of the Old Testament and the Greek of the New Testament. Some time ago, I decided to look at all of the words that described worship in both languages. In doing so, I made a discovery that surprised me and altered my whole concept of worship. I discovered that every word that described worship also described a posture or position of the body, without exception. I will give you some examples by starting at the head and working downward.

THE HEAD

In Genesis 24, Abraham's servant was sent to Meso-potamia to seek a bride for Abraham's son, Isaac. The servant did not know where he was going or whom he would meet. Without the servant realizing it, the Lord directed him to the family of Abraham's brother, which was the traditional way to seek a marriage in those times. And so, when the servant realized that the woman he met, Rebekah, was Abraham's niece, the Scripture says, *"The man bowed down his head and worshiped the LORD"* (Genesis 24:26).

Then, in Exodus, we have Moses and Aaron return-ing from the desert to bring word to the enslaved nation of Israel that God had come down and committed to deliver them from the Egyptians. After they delivered their message to the elders, we read, *"So the people believed; and when they heard that the LORD had visited the children of Israel and that He had looked on their affliction, then they bowed their heads and worshiped"* (Exodus 4:31).

In some situations, other physical postures may be difficult, but there is hardly any situation in which you cannot bow your head. For instance, when Ruth and I have a meal in a restaurant we nearly always say a rather lengthy prayer of thanksgiving. In doing so it would be impossible for us to kneel or fall face down, but bowing the head is a thing that can be done almost anywhere. I encourage you, the next time you say grace before a meal, do not keep your head upright; bow it. It makes a total difference to your whole relationship with God. It is a simple, but very significant, act.

THE HANDS

One of the world's great worshipers was David. He gave us two different postures of the hands that represent worship. Psalm 63 begins with these beautiful words:

O God, You are my God; early will I seek You; my soul thirsts for You; my flesh longs for You in a dry and thirsty land where there is no water.

(Psalm 63:1)

David was in the wilderness of Judah when he offered this prayer to the Lord.

Then he went on:

Because Your lovingkindness is better than life, my lips shall praise You. Thus I will bless You while I live; I will lift up my hands in Your name.

(Psalm 63:3–4)

The lifting up of your hands in the name of the Lord is an act of worship that is described many times in the Bible.

In Psalm 141, David described this same posture of the hands: *"Let my prayer be set before You as incense, the lifting up of my hands as the evening sacrifice"* (Psalm 141:2). Incense tells us immediately that this is about worship. In the temple, there were both morning and evening sacrifices. David was asking God to accept the lifting up of his hands as the evening sacrifice at the close of the day.

Then, in Psalm 143, David described another posture of the hands: *"I spread out my hands to You; my soul longs for You like a thirsty land"* (Psalm 143:6). Notice the language of longing for God again.

I think there is a difference in the significance of these two attitudes of the hands. When you lift up your hands, you are acknowledging God's majesty and sovereignty. When you spread out your hands, you are open to receive.

One time, when Ruth and I were at a meeting in Holland, Ruth stretched out her hands while we were experiencing some really wonderful worship. Then she said to me, "My hands are getting so heavy I cannot hold them up." The Hebrew word for glory is the same word for weight: *koved* and *chavod*. I told her, "God is putting His glory in your hands."

I tell you this because I want you to see how real God is in dealing with our bodies. We are not just disembodied spirits floating around in the air; we are people who live in very real, physical bodies. And God wants complete control of our bodies in worship.

There is another activity of the hands that I love: *"Oh, clap your hands, all you peoples! Shout to God with the voice of triumph!"* (Psalm 47:1). When we clap our hands we are worshiping God. Worship is not some rigid posture in which you sit; it is an activity of the entire body.

THE KNEES

Another person who spread out his hands to the Lord was King Solomon, when he dedicated the temple that he had built. But Solomon went a little further. He did not just spread out his hands, but he also went through into the next attitude of worship:

> *Then Solomon stood before the altar of the LORD in the presence of all the assembly of Israel, and spread out his hands (for Solomon had made a bronze platform five cubits long, five cubits wide, and three cubits high, and had set it in the midst of the court; and he stood on it, knelt down on his knees before all the assembly of Israel, and spread out his hands toward heaven).*
>
> (2 Chronicles 6:12–13)

In Daniel there is the story of when King Darius decreed that worshipers who prayed to anyone other than himself would be cast into the lion's den. This was Daniel's response to the king's written decree:

> *When Daniel knew that the writing was signed, he went home. And in his upper room, with his windows open toward Jerusalem, he knelt down*

> *on his knees three times that day, and prayed and*
> *gave thanks before his God, as was his custom since*
> *early days.* (Daniel 6:10)

Daniel had a regular practice of prayer, kneeling down toward Jerusalem (which is the way all Jews pray still, facing Jerusalem, no matter where they are in the world). So, both Solomon and Daniel knelt down in prayer.

And then in Ephesians, Paul said:

> *For this reason I bow my knees to the Father of our*
> *Lord Jesus Christ.* (Ephesians 3:14)

When Paul prayed and worshiped, one of the things he normally did was to bow his knees. Bowing your knees is an act of total submission, which is very important. I find many Christians who are not totally submitted to God. They submit when God does what they like, but when God does things differently from what they want, they complain, argue, and get upset.

One of the key words we need to learn today is *sovereign*. You don't hear that word much today, but it is a fact about God. He is absolutely sovereign. I would define it this way: God does what He wants, when He wants, the way He wants, and He asks no one's permission. The sooner you get a grip on that fact and bow your knees, the easier it will be for you to lead a victorious Christian life. God does things in our lives that we don't think He ought to do. Many of you may be holding on to some kind of complaint with Him. Be very careful of murmuring against God.

Bowing the knee is an act of worship. At some point in the future, everybody is going to do it. So you may as well beat the crowd and do it now.

> *I have sworn by Myself…that to Me every knee shall bow, every tongue shall take an oath.*
>
> (Isaiah 45:23)

At a certain point, God is going to insist that every living creature in the universe that has knees will acknowledge His total sovereignty. *"Every knee shall bow."* In Philippians, Paul indicated to whom the universe will bow.

> *Therefore God also has highly exalted Him and given Him the name which is above every name, that at the name of Jesus every knee should bow, of those in heaven, and of those on earth, and of those under the earth.* (Philippians 2:9–10)

FALLING PROSTRATE

Now we come to the most-used description of worship in the Bible – falling prostrate on your face before God. This has a distinct meaning. It means total dependence upon God. It means, "Lord, I can do nothing without You. I cannot even start." As John Bunyan once said,

He that is down need fear no fall;
He that is low no pride.
He that is humble ever shall
Have God to be his guide.

When you are face down on the floor, you have gone as low as you can go. There is only one way to go from there, and that is up.

In Genesis 17, the Lord appeared to Abraham twice. It is a very important chapter because the Lord made an everlasting covenant with Abraham and his descendants to be their God and to give them that strip of land at the east end of the Mediterranean as an everlasting possession. So, the first time the Lord appeared to Abraham (or Abram, as he was called at that time), He said,

> *"I am Almighty God; walk before Me and be blameless. And I will make My covenant between Me and you, and will multiply you exceedingly." Then Abram fell on his face, and God talked with him.*
> (Genesis 17:1–3)

Later in that same chapter, we read,

> *Then God said to Abraham, "As for Sarai your wife, you shall not call her name Sarai, but Sarah shall be her name. And I will bless her and also give you a son by her; then I will bless her, and she shall be*

> *a mother of nations; kings of peoples shall be from*
> *her." Then Abraham fell on his face and laughed.*
>   (Genesis 17:15–17)

Incredible! How could the Lord say such a thing with Sarai, or Sarah now, being well past the age of bearing children? But at the right time, it happened. Abraham grew used to being on his face before God, doing it twice in Genesis 17.

In Leviticus, there is another example of people falling prostrate before God:

> *Fire came out from before the LORD and consumed*
> *the burnt offering and the fat on the altar. When*
> *all the people saw it, they shouted and fell on their*
> *faces.*   (Leviticus 9:24)

Actually, I do not believe they could have remained standing if they had tried. They were in the immediate presence of God, the Holy Spirit. Then, later we read in Numbers,

> *So Moses and Aaron went from the presence of the*
> *assembly to the door of the tabernacle of meeting,*
> *and they fell on their faces. And the glory of the*
> *LORD appeared to them.*   (Numbers 20:6)

We continue to see examples throughout the Scriptures. Joshua fell on his face when the Commander of the army of the Lord appeared to him. (See Joshua 5:14.)

When Elijah called down fire on the sacrifice on Mount Carmel, the whole nation *"fell on their faces; and they said, 'The LORD, He is God! The LORD, He is God!'"* (1 Kings 18:39). Not one person was left standing. That is the response to the presence of God. In Ezekiel, we read,

> *Like the appearance of a rainbow in a cloud on a rainy day, so was the appearance of the brightness all around it. This was the appearance of the likeness of the glory of the LORD. So when I saw it, I fell on my face, and I heard a voice of One speaking.*
> (Ezekiel 1:28)

I question whether any man or woman who has never been on his or her face before God has ever been very close to God. You would have to search quite a way through the Bible to find any of the really great men of Scripture who had not been on their faces before God. I practice this posture of worship, not as a matter of legalism or ritual, but out of a need for security. I have found that the most secure place I know of is on my face before God. That is the way to greatness – get on your face before God.

DANCING BEFORE THE LORD

There is one more act of worship described in the Scriptures. In 2 Samuel, David had finally succeeded in getting the ark to Jerusalem after it had been captured by the Philistines and then stored for safe keeping. There had been several problems along the way. God killed a member of the first crew and they all had to learn an important lesson: the ark could only be touched by the Levites. Eventually, accompanied by all sorts of music, the ark was installed in Jerusalem, and Scripture records,

> *Then David danced before the Lord with all his might; and David was wearing a linen ephod.*
> (2 Samuel 6:14)

An *ephod* was an item of clothing that made you, in a sense, a priest. "*David danced before the Lord with all his might.*" David was a mighty man of valor, so when he danced with all his might I don't think there was any muscle in his body that was not moving. I picture him leaping up and down, giving it his absolute all. That is worship. You are not really liberated until your entire body is liberated.

But there is another side of this story:

> *Then David returned to bless his household. And Michal the daughter of Saul came out to meet David, and said, "How glorious was the king of Israel today, uncovering himself today in the eyes of the maids of his servants, as one of the base fellows shamelessly uncovers himself!" So David said to Michal, "It was before the Lord, who chose me instead of your father and all his house, to appoint me ruler over*

the people of the LORD, over Israel. Therefore I will play music before the LORD. And I will be even more undignified than this, and will be humble in my own sight. But as for the maidservants of whom you have spoken, by them I will be held in honor."
(2 Samuel 6:20–22)

And the last verse of this account reads,

Therefore Michal the daughter of Saul had no children to the day of her death. (verse 23)

And all because she despised her husband for dancing before the Lord. It is sad, but also very dangerous, to criticize people who are enjoying the Lord. They may not be proficient, and they may not be highly educated, but God likes it. He wants to be enjoyed. So be careful not to judge.

It is important to worship God with the whole body. Jesus said we must worship in spirit and in truth. Paul said, *"May your whole spirit, soul, and body be preserved blameless"* (1 Thessalonians 5:23). Remember what we learned earlier: total personality is spirit, soul, and body. You need to get your whole personality in tune with God and responding to God, as He desires.

OUR MATERIAL ACT OF WORSHIP

Another way in which we may worship God in the physical realm is in our material offerings. God wants us to see our money as something holy, something that we need to offer to Him in worship. Without doing so, our worship is incomplete. In Exodus, God gave regulations for how every male Israelite would travel to the temple in Jerusalem three times a year to offer worship and to celebrate before God.

> *Three times you shall keep a feast to Me in the year: You shall keep the Feast of Unleavened Bread (you shall eat unleavened bread seven days, as I commanded you, at the time appointed in the month of Abib, for in it you came out of Egypt; none shall appear before Me empty).* (Exodus 23:14–15)

This was part of God's ordinance for worship and celebration in the temple. They were to go at God's appointed time and in God's appointed way, and no Israelite was to appear before Him empty-handed. There needed to be an offering as part of the celebration and worship.

In Psalm 96, the psalmist said,

> *Give to the LORD the glory due His name; bring an offering, and come into His courts. Oh, worship the LORD in the beauty of holiness!* (Psalm 96:8–9)

In other words, "Do not come without an offering." In this passage we see three important facts about an offering (be it financial or anything else) to God. First, it gives glory to God. The psalmist said, "*Give to the LORD the glory due His name; bring an offering."* How are we to give glory to God? By bringing an offering.

Next it says, *"Bring an offering, and come into His courts."* Bringing an offering gives us access to God's courts. We have no right to claim access to God if we do not come with an offering. Remember the passage from Exodus: *"None shall appear before Me empty"* (Exodus 23:15). If you want to appear before God, to come into His courts, you have to bring an offering.

And third, it says to *"worship the LORD in the beauty of holiness!"* (Psalm 96:9). We are to worship Him in exactly the same context.

So, bringing an offering is a God-appointed part of our worship, and our worship is not complete until we bring our offering to Him. When we give our money to God, we are giving a very important part of our lives. Most of us would say that we put a major part of our lives into the work that brings in our income. When we offer to God the appointed portion of our income, we are really offering ourselves to God. We are actually giving Him our time, our strength, and our talents. Really, there is nothing more holy that we can offer to God than ourselves. God tells us, "If you want to come into My courts, if you want to appear before Me, if you want to give glory to Me, if you want to worship Me in the beauty of holiness, bring your offering." So, bringing an offering, worship, and holiness are all very closely connected in God's plan for your life.

GOD KEEPS AN ACCOUNT

Here is another important point that many of God's people do not fully understand: God keeps a record of what His people offer. Numbers 7 is a very long chapter – it has eighty-nine verses, and most of it is given over to describing what the twelve princes or leaders of the tribes of Israel offered to God. Each of them offered exactly the same things but the amazing thing is that each of the offerings is described in detail, item by item. God does not merely say, "The second prince offered the same as the first." He does not say, "All the twelve princes each offered this." No, Scripture goes through each and every item of each one. Now, the Bible is a very economic book – it does not waste space. So when God does this, He is illustrating to us how carefully He records what we offer to Him. Here is the account of the first prince's offering:

> So the leaders offered their offering before the altar. For the LORD said to Moses, "They shall offer their offering, one leader each day, for the dedication of the altar." And the one who offered his offering on the first day was Nahshon the son of Amminadab, from the tribe of Judah. His offering was one silver platter, the weight of which was one hundred and thirty shekels, and one silver bowl of seventy shekels, according to the shekel of the sanctuary, both of them full of fine flour mixed with oil as a grain

offering; one gold pan of ten shekels, full of incense; one young bull, one ram, and one male lamb in its first year, as a burnt offering; one kid of the goats as a sin offering; and for the sacrifice of peace offerings: two oxen, five rams, five male goats, and five male lambs in their first year. This was the offering of Nahshon the son of Amminadab.

(Numbers 7:10–17)

God kept an absolute record of what each leader offered, in specific detail, and caused it to be preserved in Scripture.

But this accounting is not just reserved for ancient Old Testament ritual. Notice in Mark how Jesus Himself carefully observed the givers:

Now Jesus sat opposite the treasury and saw how the people put money into the treasury. And many who were rich put in much. Then one poor widow came and threw in two mites, which make a quadrans. So He called His disciples to Himself and said to them, "Assuredly, I say to you that this poor widow has put in more than all those who have given to the treasury; for they all put in out of their abundance, but she out of her poverty put in all that she had, her whole livelihood." (Mark 12:41–44)

There are two points here: first, Jesus observed what everybody gave and estimated its true value; and second,

God measures what we give by what we keep. The one who put in the least, in actual value, Jesus said gave the most because she had nothing left. So bear that in mind – when God estimates what you give, He looks at what you keep.

And one final point: one day, each of us will give account to God: *"So then each of us shall give account of himself to God"* (Romans 14:12). This is the future for each one of us. The phrase, *"shall give account,"* in the original Greek, is used primarily of a financial account – not exclusively, but primarily. So, according to Scripture, every one of us is going to give a financial account to God.

God does not need our money, but He knows that our attitude about our money reveals our true attitude toward God Himself. As Jesus said,

> *"No one can serve two masters; for either he will hate the one and love the other, or else he will be loyal to the one and despise the other. You cannot serve God and mammon."* (Matthew 6:24)

We are faced with a choice. If we serve God, we do not serve mammon, the evil, spiritual force that controls and manipulates people through their attitude toward money. If our attitude toward God is right, then our attitude toward money will be right also. If we hold on to God, if we cling to Him, if we worship Him, then we will despise mammon; we will not let that evil, satanic power dictate to us. Love God or love mammon; there is no third possibility, no neutrality.

Worship is only to God. You can praise men; you can thank men; but you must not worship anybody but the Lord. This is the unique act by which we say, "God, You're our God. We worship You. We do not merely stand up and say we worship You; we kneel down and we stretch out our hands and we bow down and we fall on our faces and we worship You with all that we are and all that we have." Worshiping the Lord our God deserves the involvement of our entire being.

– 10 –

The Inevitability of Worship

Ultimately, man's choice is not *whether* he will worship, but only *whom* he will worship.

This issue is stated very clearly in the words God spoke to Israel from Mt. Sinai, words we refer to as the Ten Commandments. Here is what God said to Israel on that occasion:

> *And God spoke all these words, saying: "I am the Lord your God, who brought you out of the land of Egypt, out of the house of bondage. You shall have no other gods before Me. You shall not make for yourself a carved image, or any likeness of anything that is in heaven above, or that is in the earth beneath, or that is in the water under the earth; you shall not bow down to them nor serve them. For I, the Lord your God, am a jealous God, visiting the*

iniquity of the fathers on the children to the third and fourth generations of those who hate Me."

(Exodus 20:1–5)

I want to draw your attention to certain important points in this passage. First, God will not share worship with anyone or anything. If we worship God, we worship Him alone, and He only has the right to receive that worship. There is no other person or being or object in the universe to which we may offer our worship except to the true God.

Second, bowing down is always an indication of worship. Referring to forbidden idols, God said, *"You shall not bow down to them"* (Exodus 20:5). Bowing down and worshiping are synonymous.

The third point is very serious: the evil consequences of misdirected worship extend to our descendants. God says He will punish the children for the sin of the fathers to the third and fourth generation. This type of generational punishment does not result from other sins that men commit; this particular sin is so unique and so grievous – worshiping any other God than the true God – that God says it will be carried on in its consequences to the third and fourth generation of those who practice it.

THE GRAIN OFFERING

The book of Leviticus refers to an Old Testament material offering, but, as with many Old Testament practices, it relates to the spiritual realm and particularly to worship.

> *When anyone offers a grain offering to the LORD,*
> *his offering shall be of fine flour. And he shall pour*
> *oil on it, and put frankincense on it.*
>
> (Leviticus 2:1)

This grain offering was meal or flour that had to be ground into very small particles. As I stated before, this typifies our offering – our lives – to God. God wants our lives ground very small. He wants everything so He can deal with it without our resistance or opposition to His will.

When we offer our lives to God there are two figurative actions we must take: we must pour oil on it, and put frankincense on it. All through the Bible, oil is invariably a metaphor for the Holy Spirit. We cannot offer anything to God unless the Holy Spirit enables us to offer it.

Frankincense is a kind of aromatic gum that comes from trees. In its natural state, it is usually white in color and has no particular attractive qualities. But when it is burned, it sends forth a beautiful and distinctive aroma that typifies worship. In fact, in most instances in the Bible where you find the word describing *incense* or *scent* or *aroma*, it refers to worship.

So, when we offer ourselves to the Lord, we have to do it by the Holy Spirit, and we have to do it with worship. But something different happens to the frank-incense:

> *He shall bring it to Aaron's sons, the priests, one of whom shall take from it his handful of fine flour and oil with all the frankincense. And the priest shall burn it as a memorial on the altar, an offering made by fire, a sweet aroma to the LORD.*
>
> (Leviticus 2:2)

There has to be a priest to make the offering. He takes a small portion of flour and the oil and casts it into the fire of the offering. But – and this is very important – he includes all of the frankincense. The worship (the frankincense) goes only to the Lord. It is a sin to offer worship, to give frankincense, to anyone but the Lord. I believe this is a lesson that many high-profile Christians need to learn. In recent decades, we have seen too many distinguished, well-known figures come tumbling down in disaster and disgrace. I think one reason may be that they have sometimes permitted their followers to take a little of the frankincense and give it to the preacher.

As a preacher, I never want frankincense. Often people will approach me with flattering words, for which I am grateful, but worship goes to one person only – and that's God. Remember, anyone whom we worship becomes our god. If we worship the preacher, we are making him our god. And that is a terrible thing to do.

WORSHIP AND SERVICE

In many biblical passages relating to worship you will notice that worship inevitably leads to service. Whatever we worship, ultimately, we will serve. This is brought out very clearly in the dialogue between Jesus and Satan when Jesus was tempted to fall down and worship him. Of the three temptations in the wilderness, this was the ultimate temptation.

> *Again, the devil took Him up on an exceedingly high mountain, and showed Him all the kingdoms of the world and their glory. And he said to Him, "All these things I will give You if You will fall down and worship me." Then Jesus said to him, "Away with you, Satan! For it is written, 'You shall worship the* LORD *your God, and Him only you shall serve.'"*
>
> (Matthew 4:8–10)

Notice the order and the connection here: worship first, then serve. So many Christians try to reverse the order, but it does not work. Serving without worshiping is not the same thing.

But there is also a functional connection. The more we worship any person or thing, the more certain are the consequences that will emerge in our lives: first, the more complete becomes our commitment to the person or thing; and second, the more we will take on the identity of the person or thing. Worship inevitably leads to commitment and identification. Hence, worship is the ultimate decision, and none of us can evade it. Man was originally created to worship. He cannot change this aspect of his nature. All he can change is the direction of that worship – from the true God to a false god.

Let me give you a few examples of the false gods men commonly worship. First are actual idols. All over the world, in every culture, you will find idols of wood and stone that are worshiped. The common term we use for this is *idolatry*.

Second, people frequently worship their own physical desires and pleasures. These become their god. The name often used for the worship of pleasure is *hedonism*.

Third are money and material possessions. Millions of people around the world have made money their god. The Bible refers to this form of idolatry as *covetousness*.

Fourth would be human political leaders, such as Hitler or Lenin. It is interesting that those who reject the Bible and reject the true God with their political philosophies often end up with an alternative, human target for their worship.

Last, there are the founders of various cults and false religious ideologies. The tragic events associated with Jonestown, Guyana, and Waco, Texas, are the results of worshiping the leader of a false cult.

WORSHIP AND THE END TIMES

What do these types of false worship all have in common? They all lead to the same ultimate person: Satan.

Satan desires worship because it uniquely sets forth his claim to be equal with God. Earlier I stated that worship belongs to God alone. So when Satan can receive worship, it reasserts his claim to equality with God. This was what caused Satan's fall in the first place, as described in the book of Isaiah: *"How you are fallen from heaven, O Lucifer, son of the morning!"* (Isaiah 14:12). Morning Star and Lucifer were two of Satan's titles. In the verses that follow, the prophet reveals the inner motivation of Satan that caused him to rebel against the true God:

> *For you have said in your heart: "I will ascend into heaven, I will exalt my throne above the stars of God; I will also sit on the mount of the congregation on the farthest sides of the north; I will ascend above the heights of the clouds, I will be like the Most High."* (Isaiah 14:13–14)

Notice the one phrase that is repeated five times: *"I will."* That is the essence of Satan's rebellion, the setting of his will in opposition to the will of God. And, in the last words, we find the ultimate ambition of Satan: *"I will be like the Most High."* Again, equality with God remains the ultimate goal of Satan. And the one way he can claim it is by receiving worship, because when he does, he is identified, in a certain sense, as a god.

According to Scripture, there will be a brief period of time when Satan will come close to achieving this ambition here on earth:

Then I stood on the sand of the sea. And I saw a beast rising up out of the sea, having seven heads and ten horns, and on his horns ten crowns, and on his heads a blasphemous name. Now the beast which I saw was like a leopard, his feet were like the feet of a bear, and his mouth like the mouth of a lion. The dragon gave him his power, his throne, and great authority. (Revelation 13:1–2)

A full study of this passage reveals that the beast is a human ruler, but the dragon is Satan himself. Now look at the consequences:

So they worshiped the dragon who gave authority to the beast; and they worshiped the beast, saying, "Who is like the beast? Who is able to make war with him?" (Revelation 13:4)

This is the way human history is headed in its rebellion against God. Satan is moving and working throughout the earth, upon nations and upon political leaders everywhere with the one supreme objective of gaining their worship. Eventually, he will find a political leader whom he can so empower that this man will receive humanity's worship. And through him, Satan will receive worship as well.

Because of this, we really need to be crystal clear on one question: Whom do I worship? Who is my God? Jesus provided us with the only correct answer to that question:

Away with you, Satan! For it is written, "You shall worship the Lord your God, and Him only you shall serve."   (Matthew 4:10)

Are you willing to say that? "I will worship the Lord" and "I will serve Him only"? That is the most important decision you can make. It will determine your eternal destiny.

– 11 –

Worshiping at the Throne

Some time ago, I said to Ruth, "We do not read Revelation often enough. It is a hard book to understand, but that does not mean that we should not read it." So we read it through once, but we did not get anything out of it. We read it through a second time – but again, nothing. I said, "Never mind; it is the Word of God; we will read it." The third time, something clicked. After that, whenever Ruth would ask what we should read, she knew what I would say – Revelation 4 and 5.

Revelation 4 is about the throne room of heaven; this is the place from which the universe is run. The one key word in this chapter is the word *throne*. In eleven verses the word occurs fourteen times. Within this throne room there is one supremely characteristic activity: worship.

"Holy, holy, holy is the Lord God Almighty, who was, and is, and is to come." Whenever the living

*creatures give glory, honor and thanks to him who
sits on the throne and who lives for ever and ever,
the twenty-four elders fall down before him who sits
on the throne, and worship him who lives for ever
and ever. They lay their crowns before the throne.*

(Revelation 4:8–10 NIV)

That is the pattern of worship in heaven; they fall
down before the One who sits on the throne. I remember singing an old hymn in church: "All hail the power
of Jesus' name! Let angels prostrate fall; bring forth the
royal diadem, and crown Him . . . Lord of all." I remember looking at church-goers standing stiffly in their pews
and singing, "Let angels prostrate fall." Most would say,
"Well, that may be fine for angels, but do not ask me to
do anything so undignified!" But that is how it is done
in heaven. I know I am perfectly content to worship the
way they worship there.

In Revelation, we have a scene of the One who
sits on the throne with a scroll, which is the unfolding
disclosure of the book of Revelation. A strong angel
says with a loud voice, "Who is worthy to break the
seals and open the scroll?" (Revelation 5:2 NIV). No
one is strong enough; no one can do it in all of heaven.
John, the writer of Revelation, begins to weep because
he wants to know what is in the scroll. Then, one of the
elders says to him, "Do not weep! See, the Lion of the
tribe of Judah, the Root of David, has triumphed. He is

able to open the scroll and its seven seals" (Revelation 5:5 NIV).

John turns around, expecting to see this Lion, but only sees a Lamb, who looks as if it has been slain. John says,

> *Then I saw a Lamb, looking as if it had been slain, standing in the center of the throne, encircled by the four living creatures and the elders. He had seven horns and seven eyes, which are the seven spirits of God sent out into all the earth. He came and took the scroll from the right hand of him who sat on the throne.* (Revelation 5:6–7 NIV)

What follows is an inspiring description of the entire heavenly realm engaging in worship:

> *When he had taken it, the four living creatures and the twenty-four elders fell down before the Lamb. Each one had a harp and they were holding golden bowls full of incense, which are the prayers of the saints. And they sang a new song: "You are worthy to take the scroll and to open its seals, because you were slain, and with your blood you purchased men for God from every tribe and language and people and nation. You have made them to be a kingdom and priests to serve our God, and they will reign on the earth."* (Revelation 5:8–10 NIV)

Notice what the elders do. They fall down. And notice how our prayers come before the presence of the Lord – in golden bowls full of incense. What does incense represent? Worship! This is the first circle of worship, the four living creatures and the twenty-four elders who fall down and praise God for His mighty act of redemption through Jesus.

Then, John continues:

> *Then I looked and heard the voice of many angels, numbering thousands upon thousands, and ten thousand times ten thousand.*
>
> (Revelation 5:11 NIV)

Incidentally, this is the way the Chinese language still indicates millions – ten thousand times ten thousand is a hundred million. And then there are millions more. When you consider that one angel, in one night, could destroy 185,000 Assyrian soldiers (see 2 Kings 19:35), you wonder what we should ever have to worry about.

> *In a loud voice they sang: "Worthy is the Lamb, who was slain, to receive power and wealth and wisdom and strength and honor and glory and praise!" Then I heard every creature in heaven and on earth and under the earth and on the sea, and all that is in them, singing: "To him who sits on the throne and to the Lamb be praise and honor and glory and power, for ever and ever!"*
>
> (Revelation 5:12–13 NIV)

Every creature to the farthest bounds of the universe involved in one thing: worshiping Him. And then:

> *The four living creatures said, "Amen," and the elders fell down and worshiped.*
>
> (Revelation 5:14 NIV)

They fall down and worship Him who lives forever and ever. What an inspiring picture. The center of the universe is the throne, and it extends in ever widening circles to the utmost bounds of the universe. Everyone and everything, doing only one thing: worshiping. And who is at the center? The Lamb. What a glorious day that will be. Amen.

About the Author

Derek Prince (1915–2003) was born in Bangalore, India, into a British military family. He was educated as a scholar of classical languages (Greek, Latin, Hebrew, and Aramaic) at Eton College and Cambridge University in England and later at Hebrew University, Israel. As a student, he was a philosopher and self-proclaimed atheist. He held a fellowship in ancient and modern philosophy at King's College, Cambridge.

While in the British Medical Corps during World War II, Prince began to study the Bible as a philosophical work. Converted through a powerful encounter with Jesus Christ, he was baptized in the Holy Spirit a few days later. This life-changing experience altered the whole course of his life, which he thereafter devoted to studying and teaching the Bible as the Word of God.

Discharged from the army in Jerusalem in 1945, he married Lydia Christensen, founder of a children's home there. Upon their marriage, he immediately became father to Lydia's eight adopted daughters – six Jewish, one Palestinian Arab, and one English. Together, the family saw the rebirth of the state of Israel in 1948. In the late 1950s, the Princes adopted another daughter while he was serving as principal of a college in Kenya.

In 1963, the Princes immigrated to the United States and pastored a church in Seattle. Stirred by the tragedy of John F. Kennedy's assassination, he began to teach Americans how to intercede for their nation. In 1973, he became one of the founders of Intercessors for America. His book *Shaping History through Prayer and Fasting* has awakened Christians around the world to their responsibility to pray for their governments. Many consider underground translations of the book as instrumental in the fall of communist regimes in the USSR, East Germany, and Czechoslovakia.

Lydia Prince died in 1975, and Derek married Ruth Baker (a single mother to three adopted children) in 1978. He met his second wife, like his first, while he was serving the Lord in Jerusalem. Ruth died in December 1998 in Jerusalem, where they had lived since 1981.

Until a few years before his own death in 2003 at the age of eighty-eight, Prince persisted in the ministry God had called him to as he traveled the world, imparting God's revealed truth, praying for the sick and afflicted, and sharing his prophetic insights into world events in the light of Scripture. He wrote over fifty books, which have been translated in over sixty languages and distributed worldwide. He pioneered teaching on such groundbreaking themes as generational curses, the biblical significance of Israel, and demonology.

Derek Prince Ministries, with its international headquarters in Charlotte, North Carolina, continues to distribute his teachings and to train missionaries, church leaders, and congregations through its world-wide branch offices. His radio program, *Keys to Successful Living* (now known as *Derek Prince Legacy Radio*), began in 1979 and has been translated into over a dozen languages. Estimates are that Derek Prince's clear, non-denominational, nonsectarian teaching of the Bible has reached more than half the globe.

Internationally recognized as a Bible scholar and spiritual patriarch, Derek Prince established a teaching ministry that spanned six continents and more than sixty years. In 2002, he said, "It is my desire – and I believe the Lord's desire – that this ministry continue the work, which God began through me over sixty years ago, until Jesus returns."

Derek Prince Ministries continues to reach out to believers in over 140 countries with Derek's teaching, fulfilling the mandate to keep on "until Jesus returns." This is accomplished through the outreaches of more than forty-five Derek Prince offices around the world, including primary work in Australia, Canada, China, France, Germany, the Netherlands, New Zealand, Norway, Russia, South Africa, Switzerland, the United Kingdom, and the United States.

For current information about these and other worldwide locations, visit www.derekprince.com.

WHAT DID YOU SAY?

Your words shape your life, but it's so hard to keep your tongue under control. This book offers biblical steps so that your words will be spoken for God's glory and your blessing!

£6.99
ISBN 978-1-78263-587-1
Paperback and e-book

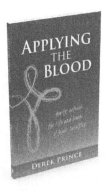

APPLYING THE BLOOD

In this essential guide for every believer, Derek Prince helps you understand and apply the power of Jesus' blood to your everyday life.

£8.99
ISBN 978-1-78263-735-6
Paperback and e-book

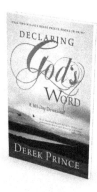

DECLARING GOD'S WORD –
A 365 DAY DEVOTIONAL

Begin your day in the presence of the Creator, rest on the truth of God's Word, and you will experience the joy of seeing Him perform miracles, signs and wonders in your life!

£14.99
ISBN 978-1-901144-51-2
Paperback and e-book

www.dpmuk.org/shop

Derek Prince Ministries Offices Worldwide

DPM – Asia/Pacific
✉ admin@dpm.co.nz
🌐 www.dpm.co.nz

DPM – Australia
✉ enquiries@au.derekprince.com
🌐 www.derekprince.com.au

DPM – Canada
✉ enquiries.dpm@eastlink.ca
🌐 www.derekprince.org

DPM – France
✉ info@derekprince.fr
🌐 www.derekprince.fr

DPM – Germany
✉ ibl@ibl-dpm.net
🌐 www.ibl-dpm.net

DPM Indian Subcontinent
✉ secretary@derekprince.in
🌐 www.derekprince.in

DPM – Middle East
✉ contact@dpm.name
🌐 www.dpm.name

DPM – Netherlands
✉ info@derekprince.nl
🌐 www.derekprince.nl

DPM – Norway
✉ xpress@dpskandinavia.com
🌐 www.derekprince.no

Derek Prince Publications Pte. Ltd.
✉ dpmchina@singnet.com.sg
🌐 www.dpmchina.org (English)
www.ygmweb.org (Chinese)

DPM – Russia/Caucasus
✉ dpmrussia@gmail.com
🌐 www.derekprince.ru

DPM – South Africa
✉ enquiries@derekprince.co.za
🌐 www.derekprince.co.za

DPM – Switzerland
✉ dpm-ch@ibl-dpm.net
🌐 www.ibl-dpm.net

DPM – UK

✉ enquiries@dpmuk.org

🌐 www.dpmuk.org

DPM – USA

✉ ContactUs@derekprince.org

🌐 www.derekprince.org